W9-CDL-260

PLOUGHSHARES

Winter 2012-13 • Vol. 38, No. 4

GUEST EDITORS
Ladette Randolph & John Skoyles

EDITOR-IN-CHIEF
Ladette Randolph

MANAGING EDITOR
Andrea Martucci

FICTION EDITOR
Margot Livesey

POETRY EDITOR
John Skoyles

PRODUCTION MANAGER
Akshay Ahuja

EDITORIAL ASSISTANT
Abby Travis

SENIOR READERS
Sarah Banse, David Goldstein,
Wesley Rothman & Abby Travis

INTERNS
Ellen Duffer &
Jordan Stillman

COPY EDITOR
Carol Farash

BLOG EDITOR
Andrew Ladd

DIGITAL PUBL. ASSISTANT
Jessica Arnold

ePUBLISHING CONSULTANT
John Rodzvilla

MARKETING ASSISTANT
Miriam Cook

Ploughshares, a journal of new writing, is guest-edited serially by prominent writers who explore different and personal visions, aesthetics, and literary circles. *Ploughshares* is published in April, August, and December at Emerson College, 120 Boylston Street, Boston, MA 02116-4624. Telephone: (617) 824-3757. Web address: pshares.org. E-mail: pshares@pshares.org.

Advisory Editors: Sherman Alexie, Russell Banks, Andrea Barrett, Charles Baxter, Ann Beattie, Madison Smartt Bell, Anne Bernays, Frank Bidart, Amy Bloom, Robert Boswell, Henry Bromell, Rosellen Brown, Ron Carlson, James Carroll, David Daniel, Madeline DeFrees, Mark Doty, Rita Dove, Stuart Dybek, Cornelius Eady, Martín Espada, B. H. Fairchild, Nick Flynn, Carolyn Forché, Richard Ford, George Garrett, Lorrie Goldensohn, Mary Gordon, Jorie Graham, David Gullette, Marilyn Hacker, Donald Hall, Patricia Hampl, Joy Harjo, Kathryn Harrison, Stratis Haviaras, Terrance Hayes, DeWitt Henry, Edward Hirsch, Jane Hirshfield, Tony Hoagland, Alice Hoffman, Fanny Howe, Marie Howe, Gish Jen, Justin Kaplan, Bill Knott, Yusef Komunyakaa, Maxine Kumin, Don Lee, Philip Levine, Margot Livesey, Thomas Lux, Gail Mazur, Campbell McGrath, Heather McHugh, James Alan McPherson, Sue Miller, Lorrie Moore, Paul Muldoon, Antonya Nelson, Jay Neugeboren, Howard Norman, Tim O'Brien, Joyce Peseroff, Carl Phillips, Jayne Anne Phillips, Robert Pinsky, Alberto Ríos, Lloyd Schwartz, Jim Shepard, Jane Shore, Charles Simic, Gary Soto, Elizabeth Spires, David St. John, Maura Stanton, Gerald Stern, Mark Strand, Elizabeth Strout, Christopher Tilghman, Richard Tillinghast, Colm Tóibín, Chase Twichell, Jean Valentine, Fred Viebahn, Ellen Bryant Voigt, Dan Wakefield, Derek Walcott, Rosanna Warren, Alan Williamson, Eleanor Wilner, Tobias Wolff, C. D. Wright, Al Young, Kevin Young

Subscriptions (ISSN 0048-4474): $30 for one year (3 issues), $50 for two years (6 issues); $39 a year for institutions. Add $30 a year for international ($10 for Canada).

Upcoming: Spring 2013, a poetry and prose issue edited by Major Jackson, will be published in April 2013. Fall 2013, a fiction issue edited by Peter Ho Davies, will be published in August 2013.

Submissions: Ploughshares has an updated reading period, as of June 1, 2010. The new reading period is from June 1 to January 15 (postmark and online dates). All submissions sent from January 16 to May 31 will be returned unread. Please see page 227 for editorial and submission policies, or visit our website: pshares.org/submit.

Back-issue, classroom-adoption, and bulk orders may be placed directly through *Ploughshares*. *Ploughshares* is also available as full-text products from EBSCO, H. W. Wilson, JSTOR, ProQuest, and the Gale Group. Indexed in M.L.A. Bibliography, Humanities International Index, Book Review Index. Full publishers' index is online at pshares.org. The views and opinions expressed in this journal are solely those of the authors. All rights for individual works revert to the authors upon publication. *Ploughshares* receives support from the National Endowment for the Arts and the Massachusetts Cultural Council.

Retail distribution by Ingram Periodicals, Media Solutions, and Ubiquity. Printed in the U.S.A. by The Sheridan Press.

Ladette Randolph photo by Tamra Turnbull. John Skoyles photo by Pamela Painter.

© 2012 by Emerson College   ISBN 978-1-933058-91-7

ISSN 0048-4474

CONTENTS

Winter 2012-13

Cover: Joe Brainard, *Untitled (Bicycle Ace)*, 2010, mixed media and gouache, collage on paper, 6" x 4". Used by permission of the Estate of Joe Brainard and courtesy of Tibor de Nagy Gallery, New York.

LADETTE RANDOLPH
Introduction

Given all of the anxiety about the future of literature in an electronic age, one thing that seems unlikely—despite the fears otherwise—is that as a culture we will stop reading. Rather, we seem to be reading (and writing) more than ever. By some counts, there were over four hundred thousand books published in this country last year, with as many as half of those self-published. In addition, there were countless stories, articles, essays, and poems published on the web.

One result of the rich supply of writing available in print and on the web is that contemporary readers are a bit dazed. Some now say they want more than anything someone they trust to direct their choices, to select from the overwhelming plenty and make recommendations. In other words, many readers are asking for someone to play the role of editor.

At *Ploughshares*, we're always struck by the number of talented writers who send us their work each year and trust us to read it with care. Our task as editors is not so much to find the "good stuff" as to make difficult choices between equally strong work. Our dedicated readers and subscribers have let us know they appreciate our making these decisions.

Although *Ploughshares* is committed to moving forward and taking advantage of the opportunities afforded us by twenty-first-century technologies—like digitally publishing our backlist and current issues for e-readers, and introducing Ploughshares Solos, a new e-book series for longer pieces—we're convinced reading carefully hasn't gone out of style.

Reading, like writing, is slow work, and we're committed to keeping it that way. It takes many dedicated screeners countless hours of reading to bring together each issue of *Ploughshares*. It's worth the time it takes. The work we publish is the work we believe will last, and will reward not only reading but also rereading. Thoughtful engagement with the world through literature is not a quick endeavor.

In fact, we believe in what might be called—if it were a movement—the Slow Reading Movement. (Or, as Maura Kelly referred to it in *The Atlantic*, the Slow Books Movement.) And as I think about it, why not start such a movement?

In a fast-paced world with more choices than we can possibly entertain, quiet contemplation has become among the scarcest of resources. Whether you do it on paper or on a screen, consider the reading of this issue of *Ploughshares* an opportunity to partake in something truly rare and valuable—your undivided time, your connection with the world not through social media, but through your own mind and imagination.

The poems selected by my coeditor, John Skoyles, and the stories and essays selected by me, range from writers whose work is appearing in a national journal for the first time, to those who have published multiple books, including a Pulitzer Prize winner. Amazingly, John Skoyles first heard Afaa Weaver read "Visit #1" in 1996. He admired the poem so much at the time he asked for a copy, which he kept all these years. For our coedited issue, John contacted Afaa on the slight chance the piece had not appeared anywhere, and it is our good fortune to have it here in print for the first time. A piece of writing that, encountered once, stays with you for years—in a world of increasingly temporary media—is the kind of work we aspire to publish.

As much as things may change in the technology of the book as we know it, there is strong evidence of an ongoing, even consuming interest in literature. This continued desire to see our lives reflected in poems, stories, and essays, is a hopeful sign. We're dedicated here at *Ploughshares* to bringing you, our reader, work we've read with care and now, with excitement, share with you.

KEITH ALTHAUS
This Candle

In the end
there is always
a little change
in the pockets,
a few suns and moons
you couldn't spend.

Nearby
the cloud
of a would-be breath
doesn't move,
reprieved
but useless.

This candle
will change all that.

Use the last bit
of air for light,
and heat the hand
that shields the eyes
and face when it gets
too close or bright.

No one speak.
The dark
will say a few words
about our friend,
leave it at that.

VALERIE BANDURA

Two Weeks

That's how much time they give you
to bribe the hall of records
for the paperwork you bribe the foreman to sign,
swearing you know nothing
and owe nothing—no loans, no debts
before you bribe a woman to sell your pots and pans,
plates, plants, rugs, and record player, so you can
bribe a dentist and a doctor
to ensure you're fit—for travel? freedom?
Who knows, but if not, another bribe
—and another and another and another
before you ask a friend to ask a friend
to meet you for the last time
on a busy street corner where you say
that that moment is the last they'll see you
because tomorrow you're boarding a train
that lets Jews, and only Jews, leave
and God willing, they'll go next.
And you say this covering your mouth
so no one overhears, so no one
will arrest your friend for being friends
with someone like you, both of you
now holding hands or wiping a cheek
or petting the other's hair.

ELLEN BASS
Restaurant

Before she told me, she let me
finish my dinner. I can still see
the pinkish cream sauce
blossoming on the china.
I didn't know yet if I could walk
when I pushed myself back from the table.
This is what gets me:
I didn't throw the stained dish against the wall.
I slipped the plastic from my wallet.
I signed my name.
No matter what we're up against,
no matter who just shot up an overdose
or broke their spine at the 5th cervical,
no matter if a child's in prison,
or turning tricks in another city,
very few people are dropping to all fours
and baying at the empty white plates.
How can you not love the human animal?
In every restaurant in Fresno, CA
the diners are opening
their cloth or paper napkins.
They spear a chunk of potato
and find as they always did
the opening to their mouths.
They chew. And they swallow.
They sip the icy water.

SHAUNA GALANTE
A Blink a Blink and Dehiscence

Now and again I get a whiff of something, the uneasy stillness before a hard and fast rain, and I can almost remember before, when I first moved in and the world was not yet fixed concretely beyond the edges of my skin. Poverty was novel then, even briefly thrilling and romantic, and it was enough to eat frozen peas at my writing desk while I transposed words with a pale blue pencil in the poems I'd saved from college.

The winter after graduation, I moved from the city to a lobstering town on the coast of Maine to write. I rented the attic of a house with two strangers, a couple in their thirties who kept separate rooms and ate every meal from shallow cardboard bowls. In the spring, I found one dead in the claw-footed bathtub. I've stayed for two years since, cleaning up, writing little. Most of my days are spent working in the kitchen of a bar and grill in town, baking the day's dinner rolls, making the soups. Financial despair still keeps me from sleep. I make only six dollars an hour at the restaurant, and we have yet to find another renter.

My grief, when I talk about Phineas, isn't affected, but it's always been mostly from obligation. *It must be hard for you,* people say. *Living there, in constant reminder.* Yes and no. For five months I had fished his SpaghettiOs out of the broken garbage disposal, stacked his bills beside Tracy's in two neat piles on the northwest corner of the kitchen table, and pressed my ear curiously to the attic floor as his amateur cello playing gave way, nightly, to the sounds of their orgasmic stuttering. Their depression was so manifest that it seemed contagious. But neither—he, especially—was more to me than an unapproachable neighbor.

I realize that I must have begun cooking to get away from writing, from my own thoughts when they became swollen too ripe to hold in the hand without bursting. I chose analogically—reductively—not realizing that neither the process nor purpose of cooking are any less elusive than those of writing. I was after a sort of vegetable fluency, a way of understanding the world by the organic and heirloom and their gradients of sweetness, and a finite vocabulary from which I could always choose, unbiased, the correct words for abstract shapes and the acts of hands upon them.

On my first day in the kitchen, I slid around on the oil-spattered tile floor in the only shoes I owned then, thin brown loafers with no traction that were all wrong for the job. Outside it had been sleeting all morning; a small handful of diners came in for lunch, and most ordered only soup. Chef gave a short talk on the breakdown of enzymes in peas during blanching and cooking past blanching, the denaturation to lack of the elemental green that makes a pea, he said, seem more like a pea. Plunging the blanched pods into an ice bath to stop the cooking, the pods floating in a Pyrex salad bowl like brilliant swimmers, he explained and I understood: the partial collapse to a bliss point of color and texture when a thing stills feels whole and honest and good. There was a wakefulness in me, and a gratitude, and I knew from the beginning that I would take everything that happened there personally.

When Phineas' parents came to gather his papers, I was struck by the resemblance that each in turn held to their own. He had been the perfect combined iteration of mother and father: her Viking tallness, her posture holding in prolonged alarm; his knuckled grip on a lavender bandanna, the long straight hairs on the backs of his hands in the light. When there was nothing else to say, I offered to help heave the rented cello to the lutherie. We had lunch, after, in a dark pub next door with small green votives on the tables, and I found myself frightened by the way they ate, slack-jawed, with an identical yellowish vacancy in their eyes. They told me, there, what had happened to him. Not one of us rose to meet the eyes of the others. Their arms were crossed low in their laps as if shamed.

I keep my eyes on the sidewalk as I walk the five blocks to work each morning, scanning for the glint of fallen change. I try to find at least one penny per day, and even one penny feels like progress. In the evening I empty my pockets into a large glass jar.

Close to the restaurant, beside the plexiglass doors of a mini-mart, there is a small hole in the cement ground, about two inches in diameter and maybe about as deep. It is filled with pennies. I'm not sure who put them there—whether it is the private collection of one of the men who beg on the corner a few yards away, or if they have never noticed it. I do not take pennies from here, but I count on them to be there as I pass the mini-mart each morning. It is a small brazen moment of comfort on my uneasy daily commute.

Thirteen months into my career I have lost eleven pounds and both of my thumbnails—one to the terrifying mandoline while shaving to tissue a thousand stalagmites of ginger; one to the implosion between front door and frame after coming home from work one night having drunk a good amount of Schlitz. I still can't cook. I am too caught up in the gentle lapsing changes of shade and viscosity, all the visual cues that say life and not-life, to remember the toast behind me before it burns. I started smoking again, as I am given no lunch hour but as many cigarette breaks as I need to take to keep from putting in my two weeks' notice. But I still feel I am moving towards a true science of the known world. I am also sleeping with the chef.

Like Phineas, he has never left Maine, and in their movements there is a sort of quietude and antelope grace, but his eyes often have a processing look that I can't imagine on Phineas' face. Mornings, we speak easily, with a respectful distance. I have replaced the attic skylight and sealed it shut with blue paint, but all the warmth still seeps from the room by dawn. The cold, early-morning smell of winter's retreat from the north will always conjure the torpidity of this time for me, our hands alight in conversation like drunken geese, the thin red glow from colored bulbs through bedsheet parachutes. His hands, so ivory white and immaculate, seem carved from bars of soap. My own, blooming bruises and splash burns, belie carelessness, mistake.

When I tell the story, not that I tell it often, almost everybody has the same reaction. I get to the part about the body, the bathwater pearly and bright as bubblegum, and what happened in the days that followed; and the listener shakes his head in sudden identification. There was a purity in Phineas' decision, a kind of mathematical grace. It seemed more to us a sordid convergence of circumstance than an act of free will. *Well no wonder. Who could blame him,* everybody says. But I dealt with the aftermath and all I saw was me. How does one mourn the finish of a foregone conclusion when one did not love the dead in life? I had to. I had to telephone the family, had to dig blond hair from the bathtub drain in my first showers after the fact. For days, my breath was shaggy from the Lysol and there was still fried chicken in the sink. I was not overwhelmed by what had happened, and I met each task with only a queasy clarity. Tracy had not left her room except to come into the kitchen one night and empty the urine from a two-gallon plastic cider jug. She offered a rehearsed defense, spat in one breath, the last words she would speak to me for several months: *You understand we all would have done the same thing.*

Tracy did not grieve conventionally, did not even attend the funeral an hour's drive north, but her behavior veered from the aloofness I had always known into a darker near-mania, in turn stoic and garrulous. She began taking sponge baths in the kitchen twice a day, one at dawn and one at 6 p.m., after both of which she'd roll a joint on the travertine floor and disappear again into her bedroom. When she slept, I lay on the kitchen floor and mapped the spiderwebbing water stains on the walls and ceiling, trying to channel the animal shock I saw in her eyes on the days that she let me catch them. She was scared, so she stayed low to the ground.

One night not too long ago, I came home from work to find her staring at the muted television, covering alternately one eye and then the other. We said a cool hello, but as I moved around the room collecting empty takeout cartons and small stray pieces of trash, she turned to me and really began talking.

"There is a theory," she began. "I mean, I have a theory."

"Oh?" I said. "I'd like to hear your theory."

"OK," she said. "Blink."

"I just did."

"Look at me," she said. "Blink."

I blinked at her. She sat cross-legged on the sofa, a news magazine on one knee. The cover story was centered on the crown scandal of the election five months prior. I wondered how long it had been since she left the house.

"Tracy?"

"What if," she said, taking a wad of bubblegum out of her mouth, twisting it in her fingers. "What if your life is a thing that is subject to a singular line of time?"

"Isn't it?" I said.

"Look, just listen," she said. "What if your life as you remember it and as it happened is the sum and the result of all the moments in which your eyes have been open?"

"OK," I said. "Sure."

"What about blinks?" she asked me.

"What about blinks?" I asked her.

"What if," she said. "What if every blink you've ever blinked in your life happened a tenth of a second later? Or a full second? So the gaps in your memory all fall at different points on the line of time? How many blinks do you think it would take for your memory to be completely different?"

"Maybe billions," I said; then, when I saw her face fall, conceded, "maybe not very many."

"Not very many at all," she said. "I think so too."

"Hmm."

"How many blinks do you think it would take for the story to actually change? For the visual information to be different enough to affect your small decisions? Or major decisions? How many blinks would it take for what happened to be different?"

I was looking at my thumbs, their running gashes and the revealed striations of tenderness. They were healing. I had blinked and the nail was caught in the teeth of the mandoline and there was blood in the bowl of ginger. I had blinked and it occurred to me that I still might not know what real pain feels like.

"I mean your life," Tracy said.

"Are you talking about Phineas?" I asked.

Her eyes turned hard. "I'm talking about eyes," she spat. "I'm talking about, fucking, the movie of your life. The progression of individual frames of your life. The organization of your entire fucking synaptic catalog. You could blink at the wrong time and everything, everything could go to shit. Or not go to shit. Everything could be fucking different." I went to her and held her. She screamed.

There is a point when peas, having reached a certain ripeness and expansive momentum, split the seams of the pod and are released into the blue. It's called dehiscence. A spontaneous rain of ovum to earth like some galactic shuddering. In a patchwork quilt fort Chef is raining kisses on me and I do not think of either of us, our persons; only the low sheet, a single green bulb in the chandelier beyond that, and the crosshatch of lashes in diminishing space. He is talking again of his new menu, arrangements borrowed from the forest just beyond town, the wilderness alive so far under the snow. There is a moment when the lines become the map and you find yourself a point in the design. The bursting, and after the burst. A quick splatter of green. I tuck his hair behind his ears and think effortlessly of the pleasant phrase *pea tendril;* not with analogic force, but sweetly, and in earnest.

At the toilet in our house I think of Phineas always. With two years gone, it is a paroxysm so reflexive that it feels muted through a screen. But today I lingered on the lip of the toilet and gave myself over to really remembering what I saw there, in the high tub a few feet away, its claws flexed over adhesive mousetraps and empty tubes of grape shampoo: his height and the braid of his arms as he bobbed there, the neatness of the knifework and the pale brown turn of his shock blond hair. Between the infinity mirrors, I recalled him, blinked optical blooms of soap scum lace in the wake of each necromantic stroke, and I felt sorry. But I cannot grieve a thing so defensible. So much a relief somehow, so much for sense, so plain.

CIARAN BERRY

The Centaur of Volos

He takes the bones of a pony,
        a pot of Earl Grey tea, a paintbrush
   and what remains of the body
where his students learned, for years,
        to name the parts, saying ulna, radius,
   tibia, skull. Saying femur, sternum,
        pelvis, clavicle.

Is this not how god made Eve
        and Adam, more or less? The one
   from clay, the other from a rib
going spare? In Wisconsin,
        it so happens that a man's making
   a centaur, joining horse withers
        to human vertebrae,

so it appears one creature belches
        out the other. Snow settles down outside
   beneath streetlights. Traffic swishes
across the interstate. For this is far
        from the city where we took the ferry
   to the Sporades, and saw, the night
        before our friends

married, a storm fork its lightning
        between islands, understanding suddenly
   how the ancients found their gods.
Small wonder that such a place
        could give birth to a creature
   all coiled muscle and sable fur,
        like the fresh bulls

I once crossed the stile and stepped
        among, their eyes deep as bog holes,
    their breath tea kettle steam in a life
that seems, by now, almost fiction,
        flies thick round the stumps of their just
    severed horns, and the blood drying
        there as black as flies,

or the sky churning above Alonissos
        when it wasn't gored by light. We fought
    that night, I can't remember why,
and in the morning fought again,
        while the garbage man's mule clicked from
    door to door its hooves. Into the room
        in which we slept,

we drew the centaur, foul-mouthed
        and ouzo-breathed, that uncouth wedding guest,
    that eater of raw flesh. Wanting to
kindle myth, wanting to do the same
        as us, the sculptor works a horsehair brush
    over croup and coffin joint, across
        the rib's dry spars.

He's trying to pin the tail to the tailbone,
        trying to suggest the weight and shade of loam
    on the back where Achilles learned to ride,
on the hand that chastised him. With this ruse
        of his, he'd have us forget the centaur's just
    a man upon a horse, another monster
        of our own bitter design.

JAMES CREWS

My Father in the Rustling Trees

I pick the lock of every knock in the night
or rasp of leaves until I hear his voice as it was
in life. Even when I want the past as charred
as these pine logs gasping for air in the stove,
heartwood turned to cinder no hand can make
whole again, I say grace for the cold scraps
memory serves, and I feel his lips pressed
to my forehead, testing for fever, then a palm
rubbing salve on my chest so when I breathe
I breathe heat, only the bedsprings wheezing
as he rises slow as smoke and switches off
the lights. His soft *Sweet dreams* sending me
into a sleep that would last and last until
the day I saw snow in his eyes, and he said
Don't be sad, and then I wasn't, I was
already listening to the trees.

Heather, 1984

There might have been other reasons Heather and I beat the hell out of each other when we performed in *The Miracle Worker* in the fall of 1984, but the best I could come up with was that she and I just weren't able to fake it.

Heather and I had been in a few plays together already, but I wouldn't say we were close. I had always liked her though, perhaps because she was so many things I wasn't—effortlessly beautiful, fair and fine-boned, funny and eccentric and completely uninhibited. The eighties were an age of shellacked hair and vivid makeup and brightly colored outfits that matched, and I loved that Heather floated down the high-school hallways in voluminous clothes in earthy, muddy tones—skirts the size of parachutes and stretched-out sweaters that hung down to her knees. Most days, she didn't wear a bra, didn't wear shoes—at least when she was inside, because this was New Hampshire after all—and up until that year, her hair had been a long, thick mess of blond waves that usually looked as though she'd just rolled out of bed. This look worked because she was so lovely, with a perfect face and eyes that were dangerous, with a mouth that said whatever she felt.

It was easy for me to assess the beauty of a girl like Heather, but I had no idea what I looked like myself. Maybe it was because the lighting in my bedroom was terrible, or because the only mirror I had sat above my dresser and I could only see one section of my body at a time as I stood on the bed, then jumped off, but I was never quite sure how all of my pieces fit together.

I wasn't ugly and I wasn't beautiful, but I wasn't sure where I fell in-between. I had a nose that seemed too big, and I had unremarkable brown hair I was constantly subjecting to unfortunate styles. I was short enough that every pound I gained or lost made my body wax and wane like the moon, and I never seemed able to create any kind of definable style from my mish-mash of thrift store finds and hand-me-downs and hard-earned purchases at O'Shea's Department Store downtown.

While I appreciated Heather's unique taste because I didn't have any myself, and while I could see in her a beauty I did not possess, Heather was not always well received by others outside the drama room. She had a reputation for being spacey and asking strange questions in class, she spoke with an accent that she seemed to have made up on her own, and her smile was sly enough it was easy to suspect she *was* laughing at you. Rumors occasionally circulated involving boyfriends she'd had or boyfriends she'd stolen and what she had done to get them, and she was open enough herself when she talked about her exploits that I found myself looking at her, thinking *She has had sex.* I suspected if I ever asked her details about those exploits, she would have filled me in completely, but of course I never did.

When Heather's mother died from cancer that past spring, many of us in the drama club went to the funeral, where it was strange to see Heather in a plain tidy dress with her hair tied back, as if she'd been fixed up and placed in a pew at the Gilford Community Church, like a delicate, perfect doll. I knew her older sister had died years before in a car accident, and I sat there for the whole service unable to pay attention to whatever anyone on the altar was saying, because I was thinking about how many pieces Heather was missing from her family. It seemed strange and unreal for her to be so alone—of course she had her dad, but this was her *mother.* And before was her *sister.* I couldn't fathom it.

I didn't always get along with my own mother—at sixteen it seemed a requirement I *not* get along with her—but more often I was happy to be in her company, as she gave me rides to one place or another and listened to me rattle on about any grave injustice I'd suffered at school or work. I wasn't always my best around her, but I couldn't imagine being without her. At the funeral, I didn't wait for the receiving line, and I didn't go to the gathering that followed the service. As if I were afraid Heather's loss might be contagious, I left as soon as I could.

A few days after school began in the fall, I saw Heather down by the drama room and was surprised to see she'd cut off most of her hair. It was strange how she still looked like Heather, but didn't.

"You cut your hair," I said, reaching up with my hand as if I might touch it.

"Yes I *did*," she said, and pulled her fingers through it so it stood straight on end, widening her eyes and making her mouth a little O, until we both laughed at how silly she looked.

"Why?" I asked, but Heather just shrugged and said, "Faith is pretty pissed."

Our drama teacher Mrs. Rupert—I'd never been able to call her Faith, though many of the drama kids did—had voiced displeasure at our hairstyle choices before. We mostly did old classics for plays—*You Can't Take It with You, Once Upon a Mattress, The Diary of Anne Frank*—and she wanted her girls to have classic hair—*long* hair. She railed against the perms and the huge bangs and the lopsided angle cuts of the eighties, so of course she'd dislike Heather's cut where the hair was just mostly gone.

"What am I supposed to do with you?" Mrs. Rupert said to Heather at the auditions. "*Miracle Worker* is in the eighteen *hundreds*. Women didn't *have* short hair. And *you!*" she said to me, using both hands to pull my layered, shoulder-length waves straight out on each side of my face. "How long will this be at show time?"

But she was our drama teacher and she could sometimes get a little dramatic. She put her stringent requirements to the side and cast Heather as Annie Sullivan and me as Helen Keller anyway.

I was happy I'd gotten such a large part, since the more time I could spend onstage, the better off I was. As my high-school years stacked up—I was a junior the year of *The Miracle Worker*—I was more in need of distraction.

Wandering the school hallways or lingering at yet another dark and smoky weekend party, I'd catch myself thinking *Get me out of here*. I was full of nameless desires I knew never could be met if I couldn't get away from Gilford, New Hampshire, so I endlessly yearned to be anywhere else.

I felt the same way when I looked at myself in that mirror at home or in the harsh lights of a department store dressing room, or when I was with a boy in a dark car thinking about what and where he might want to touch. I was desperate to get away from my body—to escape my unpredictable skin, my unmanageable hair, my doughy flesh. I felt like a picture colored in a book by a kindergartener who couldn't stay in the lines—all over the place and sloppy, something to rip out and throw away.

I forgot these anxieties when I worked on the school newspaper with our adviser, Mr. Proudfoot, when I talked in Mr. Sargent's English class about Thoreau and Emerson and Emily Dickinson, and especially when I was up on stage, pretending to be someone else. It was so much easier when my lines were written for me and I knew exactly what to say, when I knew from the beginning how things would end, one way or another.

And what about Heather? Why did she want to go on stage? She might know she was beautiful—she certainly acted like she knew—and she might be comfortable enough with her body and her desires, but maybe, too, she knew that people gossiped about her or made fun of her clothes, or knew they said she was just plain crazy. And then there was her mother and her sister—there was no escape from that. Was that what she was trying to forget? We spent hours together every day for almost three months of rehearsals and not once did I ask.

Heather and I hardly talked at all in rehearsal—at least not to each other—but that had a lot to do with the play. There was plenty of dialogue in *The Miracle Worker* showing how Helen came to be this untamed creature, pushing her family to its wit's end, and how Annie's stubborn resolve to reach Helen had a lot to do with her own history—losing her mother and then her brother, going blind herself, her own sight restored just before she took on the task of being Helen's teacher—but all this dialogue went on around me, above me.

In pretending to be deaf and blind, I was in my own world for all of these scenes—present enough to connect with my cues, but otherwise completely removed. It was easy to muffle the sounds around me and disengage. I'd employed this skill plenty during those times I yearned to be anywhere else. I was engaged in English class and especially when I worked on the newspaper—talking about music reviews or special-feature ideas, editing stories on the school's new computers and shouting out pun-filled headlines just to make Mr. Proudfoot groan in mock distress—but everywhere else, I'd go behind this gauzy curtain, emerging only after my name was repeatedly called.

It was easy to do, especially at parties I went to with my best friends Holly and Nancy, where we'd drink or I'd smoke cigarettes, and the alcohol would help drop that curtain more thickly over our eyes, the smoke give us something to hide behind. Other than shouting to each other, "I love this song!" or raising our eyebrows at the antics of people more drunk than we were, we never really said much. There was no point in talking or looking each other in the eyes; it was enough just to be there together.

I didn't look Heather in the eyes either; as Helen I wasn't supposed to anyway, and Heather wore these smoky spectacles that Annie needed to protect her eyes, so there was nothing there to see. And of course our scenes together were almost entirely silent. Heather had a few lines here and there where Annie is talking to herself or where she's spelling out all the sign language letters that she's pushing into Helen's palm— C-A-K-E, D-O-L-L, W-A-T-E-R—but the rest of our interaction was entirely physical, and that interaction quickly escalated.

The scenes began sedately enough where Annie is feeding Helen's insatiable curiosity, trying to get her to connect the words she's spelling into Helen's palm with the objects Helen is touching or smelling or eating. But you'd think the stage directions for the rest of our scenes were for a series of bar fights or boxing matches—HELEN *hits* ANNIE *squarely in the face;* HELEN *waits, tensed for further combat;* ANNIE *firmly pins* HELEN *by her wrists;* HELEN *retaliates with a roundhouse fist;* ANNIE's *hand leaps out in a forceful slap.* There was no question of what we were supposed to do, and the reason why was in the play as well.

"Obedience is the gateway through which knowledge enters the mind of the child," the stubborn Annie says, but Helen is so wild that the obedience comes with a price. It's only after Annie takes Helen away from her family—to a small summer cabin tucked away in the woods where Helen has no idea how close to home she still is—that Annie is finally able to break through. But until that moment arrives, the battle gets intense.

Initially, Heather and I joked as we played at throwing each other around, as we became less shy about touching each other so much, because she and I were physically so close in scenes that our bodies were almost always connected in some way. Heather would sign letters into my palm and I would sign them back, or Heather would hold my hands as I touched her face and lips and hair. And when the stage directions called for fighting, we'd have to grab each other by the shoulders and wrists and waists; then we'd grunt and sweat as we pulled each other off chairs or away from tables and onto the floor.

If Heather had been a boy, this would have been too intimate, too intense. I never could have stood being touched that way. Once on stage it all seemed natural, especially after Heather and I knew our blocking and the order of the action. Mrs. Rupert initially stopped us often to refine her directions, interrupting our momentum, but the closer it came to the performances, the more she just let us go. Adrenaline pumped and we stopped holding back as we wrestled and pinched and slapped; I was hardly conscious of Mrs. Rupert watching and taking her notes, of the cast waiting for the next scene to begin, of the techies fine-tuning the lights and the sound. I went to another place in those scenes, a place that was black and empty and noiseless—and I wasn't sure if I'd dragged Heather there or she'd dragged me, but we were locked there together nonetheless.

I'd been pulled into a darkness on stage—that same place I tried to go when I drank too much at parties or listened to music alone in my room. But being on stage with Heather beating the hell out of me was even better, because it left me with bruises that proved the pain I felt was real.

Mrs. Rupert wasn't clueless—she was pleased with the power of the scenes but said every night she was afraid we were getting hurt. And every night Heather and I repeatedly said we were fine as we sat there exhausted, our faces shining and our hair damp with sweat, and Mrs. Rupert just looked at us skeptically before moving on.

And for those three weeks of the most intense rehearsals, I became increasingly fascinated with my battered body. At night in my bed I'd feel where the bruises were, assessing how much more of me had been damaged. Even when I'd played basketball and field hockey, even when I'd flown over my handlebars and into a ditch across from Patti Harding's house in fifth grade because I'd tried to go all the way down the hill to her house without using my brakes, I don't think I ever got as banged up as I did in *The Miracle Worker*.

I liked tracing the different bruises, following their uneven perimeter or probing their center to feel that slight sting of pain once again. In the shower every morning, patting myself gingerly with a towel after stepping out, I'd monitor the changes in color, from purple to black to green, looking closely for the rust-colored spots of dried blood beneath the skin or the bright spidery veins that shone beneath sallow yellow.

It was a strange relief knowing those bruises were there, as if how I felt—big and obvious and painfully desperate to get away from my school, my town, myself—was now how my body looked. It made me wonder how Helen had felt—because of course she'd had bruises of her own, far more than I'd ever know. What had she wondered about how the world had suddenly changed around her? When she was stuck only with Annie, unable to understand or communicate, knowing only that the touch of her mother had disappeared? She must have been wild with fear and sadness.

And what of Annie, who understood fear and pain as the only way to reach Helen and make her obedient, though Annie's own life had already seen enough loss and pain?

I wanted to keep these bruises a secret—like my lies to Mrs. Rupert about not being hurt, I didn't want to worry anyone—and it didn't seem that hard. In the fall in New Hampshire, long sleeves and pants are the norm anyway, and I was pretty sure no one noticed. But a few days before our first show, I was sitting in the cafeteria with Nancy and Holly, and they asked me if I'd be ready for opening night.

"Yeah, I just hope I survive it," I said and pushed up my sleeves to show them my arms, turning them this way and that so they could see how beaten up I was, telling them all about what Heather and I had been up to.

"Oh," Holly said. "I'm so glad. We couldn't figure it out."

"You knew?" I said.

"Yeah," Nancy said. "We knew something."

"So that's all it was," said Holly.

"That's all it was," I said.

I guess part of me knew that even long sleeves get pushed up now and then, even a bruise can creep its way past a collar, but it was sad to me they'd said nothing, though of course I knew they cared. It just meant that what I believed to be true was true—if you don't say something, no one will ask you. If you don't ask—and you hardly ever ask—no one will tell you anything. But then Mr. Proudfoot spoke to me as I was trying to lay out the feature pages for the newspaper before running off to our last dress rehearsal.

"How are the battle scars?" he asked. "Will you make it this weekend without going to the emergency room?"

I looked at him in surprise. Mr. Proudfoot had a reputation for being a little omniscient—a reputation he carefully cultivated as our journalism adviser—but I was still taken off guard. "What?" I said.

"You and Heather are quite the method actresses, aren't you?"

"I don't know," I said, blushing at what I thought might be one of those rare compliments Mr. Proudfoot parceled out about two times a year, though it always was hard to tell when he was joking.

"You have been *gone* these past couple months," he said. "Here but not here. Like you really couldn't even see or hear anything going on around you."

"Oh?"

"Yes," said Mr. Proudfoot. "But after this weekend, I expect you back. Understand?"

I wasn't sure I did, but this time I knew Mr. Proudfoot wasn't kidding.

"OK," I said.

The day of *The Miracle Worker*'s first performance, I went early to the drama room for some peace before everyone else arrived. Heather was already there, and she looked up from where she was sitting on the floor, her skirt pushed between her legs and one hand lingering over a large, dark bruise just above one of her knees.

"I did that," I said, pointing to the bruise.

"Yes," she said, and laughed. "Thank you very much."

I walked over, sliding down the wall to sit next to her on the floor. "Look," I said, and pushed up my sleeves once again, showing my battle scars as well.

Heather nodded and held her arms out, showing me first the inside, then the out, before reaching down to pull her skirt up farther, lifting one bruised leg, then the other. Her banged-up body was remarkably similar to mine.

"I'm sorry," I said.

"Nothing to be sorry about," Heather said, pulling her skirt back over her knees. "It's not your fault, it's just the play."

I leaned my head back against the wall. Maybe she was right, but it felt like it was my fault. Mine and hers and Mrs. Rupert's. And it was Nancy and Holly's fault too, as well as everyone else's who never said anything or did anything except sit back in the dark and watch life play itself out, as if it were make-believe.

"But it hurts, doesn't it," I said.

Heather laughed out loud, that laugh of hers I loved because she saved it for situations where it rarely made any sense.

"It does," she said. "It really hurts a *lot*."

CARL DENNIS
Laundry Day

All one needs to belong to the company
Of the truly grateful is to feel grateful,
Just as I felt when, retrieving a sock
This afternoon from behind the dryer,
I found the book you lent me
Four years ago, two years before your heirs
Sold off your library. Did you ever wonder
What had become of it, you who lent books
To so many friends that you couldn't remember
Where each one went. Four years,
And its pages are still legible
Though dark with mildew.
A book on what has to be done at once
To save the biosphere from calamity,
How best to persuade our species
It's time to swallow some bitter medicine.
Four years on the floor behind the dryer,
And with every year it's become more true.
For your sake, if not the planet's,
I ought to do more than vow
To search for a cleaner copy
And put it back into circulation.
I ought at least to write a rebuttal
To the article in last night's paper
On the need of our species to adjust
To its new environment, as the fittest
And shrewdest have always done.
No matter if my letter makes no difference
So long as I believe you'd endorse it.
For your sake I should write it this evening,
Your gift open beside me as a guide

To resisting the voice of moderation,
The fatal charm of compromise.

CARL DENNIS
Loitering

"No Loitering" reads the sign by the school.
But what about a school that offers courses
In loitering as an art, each class designed
To break another link in the argument
That we ought to be somewhere else by nightfall,
Ought to start now if we're to arrive on time
For the meeting of those in need of a truth
We've distilled over years in private study.
It's likely they know already what we know.
Better stay here, loitering at dusk in the garden
A moment more, while the resident birds and squirrels
Settle themselves in the boughs of the linden
And the roiled thoughts of the day grow quiet.
This is the hour when the lover loiters on the sidewalk
Across the street from his sweetheart's house,
Waiting to see a light go on in her study
So he can imagine her reading his letter
In a mood that prompts her to a kind reply.
This is the hour when a daughter loiters
By her mother's grave, in the final moments
Before the gate of the graveyard is locked for the night.
Here's a last chance for her mother's spirit
To make its presence felt unmistakably.
Gone to a better world, the minister said.
But her mother wasn't looking for an alternative.
How happy she would have been to loiter in this one
An extra summer, plus an extra day.

HILARY VAUGHN DOBEL

Patience

It was a straw light, a blond
light, a water light in the window
when I looked outside and saw it was
still daylight, flooding the hot, white

room of her death that had been
the hot, white room of her maternal
loneliness. The heel of my hand
hard on her sternum as her heart,

in its irregular quiver,
twitched below—as I cracked each
rib from its mooring with my first
compression, a terrible

champagne pop, and almost stopped
upon that first violation. It grew
no lighter or darker, until a higher-
up told me no more. The body sighed.

They do that, sometimes.
What happened after I closed
her mouth and eyes, peeled, one
by one, the leads from her chicken

flesh, after I rebuttoned her blouse
and returned her to bed like a girl,
was not my business, incense
or crematorium. She was the first

recalcitrant corpse of spring,
and I feel that same nausea,
now, on a bus heaving through
Connecticut just south

of the Massachusetts border—
the same icicle snap in every screech
and jostle, as the wind boils outside,
as my head sinks and I think of you.

Run Away, Join Circus

When I woke, makeup-smeared and sallow,
everyone was gone. Greasepaint smooth
in the new line of my cheek and corset-bruises

on my hips, first warm day of the year. A false
eyelash settled like a moth on my collarbone.
They loved me on the high wire last night

in my spangled tights all done up as the queen
of diamonds, and when I looked down it was
a fanged kaleidoscope. Tits hiked up like two big

jokes, I smiled with a throwing-knife
between my teeth and waved from beneath
the shade of an elephant. I slept on an old-country

quilt that smelled of ginger and sweat
between the Siamese twins and a Latvian
acrobat who wiped my face with geranium oil,

then rested his lips on my shoulder. I never thought
the striped canopy would be gone in the morning,
leaving me a bald sky screaming desert gold

as night began to fade. I followed the road
back to town, to the window I knew
I could make it in through before the rest of them

woke up, if I would hurry and shake the tinsel
from my hair, rub fuchsia from my mouth, tie
the chain back around my ankle, swallow the key

to wait, again, for the sound of a calliope.

BARRY GIFFORD
The Wicked of the Earth

Roy and Jimmy Boyle were shooting pool on a rainy Saturday afternoon in Lucky's El Paso when Mooney Yost, a Lucky's regular, came in and sat down on a bench near the boys' table. Yost was about fifty years old, a fin and a sawbuck hustler who was always kind to Roy and his friends. He liked to tell slightly off-color jokes. "What's the lightest thing in the world?" he'd ask, then answer himself: "A man's penis—it only takes a thought to lift it." He didn't look happy sitting on the bench, though, and after Roy and Jimmy finished their game, they sat down on either side of him.

"What's wrong, Mooney?" Jimmy asked. "Your dog get run over?"

"Dogs don't dig me," Mooney said. "They take one sniff and head for the hills. Must be something in my blood reminds 'em of bein' beaten in Egypt back in the days of the pharaohs. No, I was just talkin' to my sister, Rita, in Peoria, and she told me that our mother's last husband died a bad death. He was her fourth or fifth, not even my mother remembers anymore. His name was Reno Mott. He was Rita's stepfather, she's twelve years younger than I am, and I was gone by the time our mother married him. Rita's father was my mother's third or fourth husband, a cat burglar named Slippery Elmo Daniels.

"Anyways, this last husband had been divorced from our mother for more than twenty years. He wasn't smart or rich or even very good lookin', but my sister says he was always nice to her. I met Reno Mott a few times but I had no use for his ass. Despite his religious dishonesty, constant lies and penny-ante swindling, he never made even a modest living and lost every cent my mother had, including whatever I give her or Rita did.

"He remarried, my sister said, and he and his new wife lived in a trailer on the outskirts of Phoenix, Arizona. He worked odd jobs, Rita told me, the final one for a messenger service deliverin' small packages in his old Buick that didn't have headlights. His wife worked as a bank teller. Reno kept at it until he was eighty; then his vital organs began to go one by one. Rita went to see him in the hospital a few days before he died. Drove all the way from Peoria, Illinois, to Phoenix. She's a good girl, Rita. He was hooked up to a few machines and he was scared. He told my sister that he'd lived a bad life, cheatin' people all the time, pretending to be a big shot, and failing at everything he tried. Mott lost his messenger job after he drove into a kid on a bicycle and killed him. The police let him off because the kid had darted out from an alley or a side street without lookin' to see if any cars were comin'. It was typical of his bum luck, Mott told Rita. He'd done everything the wrong way, he said, and now he was about to die without money, love, or peace of mind.

"My sister talked to his wife after he died, and the woman told her it had been a real ugly deal. She was in the hospital room when the nurses pulled the plugs. He stood up next to the bed and howled, 'I don't want to die! I've led a mean life, I've hurt everyone I've ever known. I've stolen money from children, I've killed people! Now I'm goin' to hell, I have to go to hell and I'm afraid! Oh, Lord,' he cried, 'you know me only as one of the wicked of the earth, and my flesh trembleth for fear of thee!'

"Reno carried on like this, his wife said, for more than a minute before he collapsed to the floor and was pronounced dead. His eyes were rolled back in his head and his mouth was open. Almost all of his teeth were gone. His tongue was green and hung out of one side of his mouth. Rita told his wife that Mott had been nice to her when she'd been a young girl. The woman thanked her for saying so, and said once Reno had read about a boy who'd been hit in the head and lost his ability to remember anything after that. The child's mind was frozen in time. Not only could he not remember anything new, but also he did not even recognize himself in the mirror as he grew older. Reno thought that would be the perfect way to live, with nothing terrible in your mind to haunt you forever.

"When my sister told our mother that Reno Mott had died, she said, 'I thought he died years ago.' Rita said he believed he was going to hell and was afraid to burn. 'I'm not surprised,' my mother said. 'He never did any good in his life.' 'He was always nice to me,' said Rita. Our mother looked at her and said, 'I don't believe you.'"

Mooney stood up, stretched his lanky frame, and said, "Be thankful, boys, you don't have a Reno Mott messin' with you. Guess I'll see if I can scare up a game of one-pocket."

"I don't really feel like playin' anymore," said Jimmy.

"Neither do I," said Roy.

They racked their cues, walked to the door, and pulled their jackets up over their heads before going out into the rain.

PETER EVERWINE

A Story Can Change Your Life

On the morning she became a young widow,
my grandmother, startled by a sudden shadow,
looked up from her work to see a hawk turn
her prized rooster into a cloud of feathers.
That same moment, halfway around the world
in a Minnesota mine, her husband died,
buried under a ton of rockfall.
She told me this story sixty years ago.
I don't know if it's true but it ought to be.
She was a hard old woman, and though she knelt
on Sundays when the acolyte's silver bell
announced the moment of Christ's miracle,
it was the darker mysteries she lived by:
shiver-cry of an owl, black dog by the roadside,
a tapping at the door and nobody there.
The moral of the story was plain enough:
miracles become a burden and require a priest
to explain them. With signs, you only need
to keep your wits about you and place your trust
in a shadow world that lets you know hard luck
and grief are coming your way. And for that
—so the story goes—any day will do.

ONA GRITZ

Retelling

The sun was nothing more than an orange
the day Lisa ran for the ice cream truck.
It was small and even if it held sweetness,
even if it seeped Vitamin C, it couldn't stop
the car from barreling down Mott Avenue,
couldn't shine enough to show the driver
the eight-year-old girl dashing in front of his
Pontiac so that his foot would choose the brake.
The trees that saw it happen were no more
than rakes upended. They had no leaves
to form shadows. They had no song.
For a long moment, doorknobs
were merely ornamental. Those of us still
in our houses stayed in our houses.
I, six at the time, kept watching cartoons
while the sun watched over us and the trees
turned into notebooks so the story could change.

KARL TARO GREENFELD
Strawberries

In the days before the wedding, as caterers and florists and seamstresses and bakers and even sommeliers and fromagers and charcutiers made appearances at the Maison ClosDennis, there were two of us who were irrelevant to the preparation of the proceedings. One of them, and this anyone could have predicted, was me, the boyfriend of Lily-Anne, younger sister of Anna-Marie, the bride. The other redundancy to the planning process—physically and mentally unnecessary, I should say, but financially integral—was Matheus, or Matti, as he had asked me to call him, the father of the bride.

For a while, we passed the time in the vast living room of Maison ClosDennis, a chamber that was roughly octagonal with a large, colonnaded fireplace the size of a minivan, the mantle taller than me. The ceiling was supported by beams of a type I had never seen before, made of solid brown stone, and just a half-meter below those beams were immense dormer windows, the upper halves of which were stained glass and appeared to have been looted from some even more ancient structure, a Frankish cathedral perhaps. The windows faced north, overlooking a steep, wooded slope descending to the Meuse River, or the Maas, as German Matti called it. The living room, on the first floor, to the left as you entered the house, past the chapel— the house had a chapel—was a strategically astute spot to plant ourselves. It was far, far away from the kitchen and south-facing balconies and so required a dedicated, determined trip to come and visit. We spent the first day watching a golf tournament, I believe it was the Ryder Cup, and then the next day, there was an F-1 race, similarly dull. We drank wine from Matti's cellar and snacked on these local versions of Japanese rice crackers of which Matti was fond.

The wedding was to be held one week hence, in another château not far from here, on a hill that I understood to be, from Matti's gesturing, to the Northeast. Four hundred guests were expected at the ceremony, two hundred at a dinner, and then five hundred were to convene for the reception and party. There were also various rehearsal dinners, bridesmaids' events, bachelor parties, and so forth, each of which had to be planned and organized and, of course, paid for. Every half-hour or so, one of the women—Matti's wife, Baumy, or one of his daughters, Lily-Anne or Anna-Marie, or his daughter-in-law, either Petra or Monique—would enter, holding a brochure or a photograph or a laptop computer on which would be a representation of a last-minute detail not yet attended to. They were checking with him, usually regarding price.

He would slide on a pair of wire-frame reading glasses, pretend to study the matter at hand, and then say, in German, "*naturlicht.*"

After the woman left, he would turn to me and say, in English, which he spoke waveringly, "David, I care not so much about these small items." And he would shake another Gauloises Red from the pack and light up and watch Colin Montgomery make his approach on seventeen.

At one point, we were watching the F-1 race at Nürburgring on German television when there was a crash, a driver for Jaguar hitting the rail and one of his tires bouncing back onto the track and causing a driver for Honda to spin into hay bales on the inside of the turn. The German announcers were shouting excitedly, and the camera panned to the pit crews watching the accident on their closed circuit screens. When the Jaguar driver—it was Eddie Irvine—emerged from his car, he was stamping his feet, furious.

"David," said Matti, "This driver is very angry. The racing host, he says the Jaguar motor was sabotaged in the night before by the Ferrari team. It's a big problem."

Periodically, one of Matti's sons would arrive, both of whom now worked in the company that Matti had founded and then sold. Both sons, of course, knew to keep as far as possible from the preliminary to the wedding, and so their appearances would be brief, one cigarette, a quick beer, and they would be back in their high-performance Teutonic sedans and gone, leaving me and Matti to our drinking and television-watching until our inactivity finally roused the anger of the womenfolk. Over lunch one afternoon, led by Baumy, a formidable German woman of Swabian descent who, among other credentials, was a licensed pilot who had survived the crashing of her own plane, they lashed out. Frustrated at Matti's indifference to the proceedings, the mounting preparations, the imminent arrival of guests, many of whom would be quartered here in the château and would require feeding, bathing, etc. Baumy began to nag him in German to do something, anything, which Matti stoically didn't respond to, eating his Moutaschen dumplings, which were excellent, and sipping his Alsatian white.

His daughters joined in, Lily-Anne heaping her approbation on me.

"What am I supposed to be doing?" I asked.

She actually suggested cleaning. There was a staff who did that, I pointed out, but there was no logical response; it was our inactivity that had roused their ire, and nothing but mindless activity would assuage them.

Matti suggested we drive to Luik to look for strawberries.

I had first met Matti three years ago, when I turned up at his summer-house in Mallorca as the new paramour to his younger daughter. Lily-Anne and I had met in New York, where we still lived. Neither of us were the type to spend much time considering our relationship or wondering where it was going. We were both, in that way, superficial, pleased enough to be with someone we found attractive and in no way objectionable.

And when on occasion I did try to figure out Lily-Anne, I didn't make much progress. She was unfathomable to me, beautiful, tall, with unsteady, accented English. She could be surprisingly sweet, but on those occasions when she became angry, she became a sullen, sucking force, creating gravity that could consume all the happiness around her. What did she think about when she was neither sweet nor angry? I had no idea. But as I watched her, I realized she was perhaps thinking nothing at all.

Her prosperous German family provided her what mysterious depth she had.

I was the first American boyfriend, also the first one of Jewish descent; still, Matti had no reason to be anything more than civil with me. How many previous boyfriends had his daughters brought home over the years? They were both pretty girls, taking after Baumy, and it must have been a steady procession. Yet he was gracious, friendly, and for some reason seemed to take a liking to me, which I reciprocated. He had grown up in the Alsace, during the war when the region was German, and then after the war when it was occupied by France. He understood a half-dozen languages, but was barely fluent at speaking any of them save German. He had been an exceedingly handsome man, tall, narrow-faced with a cowboy squint, mustache, strong chin, looking a little like James Coburn in his prime, and relied on his stolidity and stern expression to bluff through business meetings. And he had demonstrated enough aptitude in mathematics to earn an engineering degree and then a job at AGFA. He stayed there for three years, and then he invented his machine.

I had seen the machine a half-dozen times, when he took me to visit his factories. There were several such plants, spread all over the Benelux region. The machine was vast, the size of two cargo containers, and took a half-dozen men to operate. It involved a steel frame, hanging from which was an engine of some kind, and this engine drove several massive spindles and bobbins that pulled some sort of fiber in long, thick belts up and through a furnace or oven and then through a spraying apparatus, until the fiber was recollected on other bobbins, presumably then different in some way from when it had gone in. Matti had tried numerous times to explain to me what this machine did, but I never quite understood. I know it is vast, and very loud, and that he built his factories around these machines, and he sold these machines, to other men who built factories, all over the world. And if you bought a machine from Matti, then you also bought a many-year service contract from his company. These contracts, and the factories and the company he had built and sold, allowed Matti to retire at fifty and live in a château.

Matti loved cars, and each of the two times a year that I saw him, among his first questions would be, "David, what is your favorite car?" I'm not sure anyone had asked me that question since the third grade, yet Matti took the question seriously.

The first time he asked me, shortly after our introduction, I answered, Audi A6; he shook his head, disappointed. "David, that is a good car, sure, but it shouldn't be your *favorite* car." He pointed out that a favorite car had to be, say, an Aston Martin, he had one of those, or an Austin-Healey, he had two, or a Rolls-Royce Corniche, he had one, or a Jensen, or Jaguar, and so forth. Your favorite car, in other words, had to be something expensive and difficult to maintain, exotic, preferably English, but certainly not a production sedan like the Audi A6.

Matti currently had two favorite cars, for example, a Morgan 4/4 and an Austin-Healey 3000, and he pored over collectors' magazines looking for pristine examples of them. He kept his car collection in a warehouse in one of his former factories in Belgium, the terms of the sale of his company allowing him to keep his cars stored there until his passing.

So now, before going to Europe with Lily-ann, I always went online and did a quick search to find a new favorite car—Matti would be very disappointed if I had the same favorite car as last time we met—and so when he asked, I was always prepared.

"1958 Jaguar XK150S Roadster."

He would nod, pleased by my choice.

For our trip to Luik, he said we would take his Aston Martin DB5, the famous James Bond roadster, which was "roughly 18 kilometers per hour faster than the Jaguar XK." But, he warned, "She is thirsty, like all Aston Martins."

I asked if he had heard anything more about the F-1 scandal, the Ferrari sabotaging of the Jaguar car.

He laughed. "David, I was fooling with you. No such incident occurred."

"You made that up? The whole thing?"

"For amusement!"

He deftly began manipulating the ball-handled gearshift, and soon we were making noisy progress along the highway that followed the Meuse to Luik, or Liège as the Francophone Belgians would call it.

Straddling the Meuse, which breaks into two branches as it passes through the city, Liège was a depressed, former industrial city that had fallen on hard times in the 1960s and never recovered. Its heyday had been the mid-nineteenth century, the city's grand architecture dates from that period, neoclassical municipal buildings, Gothic cathedral, and scaled-down versions of Haussmann-like apartment buildings, such as you would find in Paris. It had once been a prosperous place, when the local textile and mining industries were still globally competitive. But now, driving through the city's narrow streets, one felt as if a residue of dust had settled onto the place, lending the grand buildings and bourgeois apartments the air of fancy garments left too long in an attic, forgotten finery.

It had a thriving red-light district, a reputation as a way station for human traffickers moving their product from east to west or south to north, and, apparently, a burgeoning fresh-fruit market where one could buy truck farm strawberries.

Matti pointed out to me the Liège post office, a neobaroque palace with numerous towers, gables, porticos, and at least three weathervanes and a four-sided clock, each side of which told a different time. The whole structure, occupying a city block and including accompanying parking lot, had been on sale, for the last five years, for one million euros.

He parked next to the post office, and we wandered in a light drizzle down cobblestoned streets toward, I assumed, the market where we could collect those strawberries. Instead, Matti stopped at a café with two abandoned sidewalk tables with mismatched chairs, and pointed inside a dark, sour-smelling doorway from which emitted a noisy, boisterous singing. He suggested we have a drink.

We stepped into the wood-paneled café. In the back corner opposite the door, past a lectern-high, heavy oak bar, was the source of the song: an elderly man in cowboy boots, jeans, large antler belt buckle, Pendleton shirt, and structurally unsound pompadour—it was tall but seemed to lack sufficient follicles to keep standing, this old man having built the coif from just a few strands and, presumably, a vast amount of hair spray and gel. Despite his Old West–themed outfit, he was singing a droning French song, about, if I am correct, a man waiting for his love at a carousel? Or somewhere that had a name that sounded like "carousel"? His voice was a low, steady growl, and he took frequent drags from his cigarette, and when the waiter brought him another *demi* of beer, he took a sip of that. Behind him, a bespectacled piano player plinked steadily on an old upright in accompaniment, and on a bench alongside the singer, three old ladies and one man periodically wavered to the unsteady beat, or quietly joined in for a verse or two, before returning to sorting through sheet music piled on the table in front of them.

There was wood paneling halfway up the walls, and above that were tacked hundreds of black-and-white photographs. I couldn't tell if these were famous people—other countries' celebrities always being the most confusing category of fame for me—or if they were locally renowned, or if these were photographs of these very same people in the bar right now, only younger.

Matti ordered us each a demi. He laid his pack of Gauloises Red on the table, and we smoked and listened to the man's song. Seated at another table were two chubby little boys, one of whom was preoccupied with a handheld game device, and the other was drinking bright red soda from a glass. Their faces struck me as familiar; they looked almost porcine with pinkish flesh, puffy lips, thick noses, round eyes, large foreheads, scant hair. I realized I had seen their like in the paintings of Pieter Brueghel. In fact, the sizable pompadour on the singer aside, everyone in here looked as if they had stepped out of one of his canvases.

I drank my beer, and immediately Matti secured for us two more. And then two more.

There was more singing, this by an elderly woman in Burgundy skirt and tan top. She had the lowest hanging breasts I had ever seen, large teardrop-shaped sacks descending over the belt of her skirt. Her song, from what I could gather, was a lament about lost love. Other patrons, Matti included, lustily joined in for the refrain: "*ooooooooh, j'ai pleuré.*"

While she was singing, I noticed the chubby boys staring at me and whispering to each other. I didn't look like anyone else there, but I'm not sure why my appearance should have elicited any notice. I have never been described as looking particularly stereotypically Semitic, if there is such a look. I don't know if my appearance was what the children were reacting to, but over the high notes of the piano, I thought I heard one of the boys muttering "*juif.*" Or was I imagining that? After the beer, and amid all the racket, I couldn't tell. But the next time I caught the boys staring at me, I gave them a sudden glare back, and then made a quick, seated lunge, nothing more than an elaborate flinch, really, but it was enough to cause the one drinking red soda to leap up and start crying. I felt immediately guilty for my reaction; he couldn't have been more than ten years old.

Matti had ordered for us two more demis, and I tried to refocus on the singing, but I noticed the crying boy now being comforted by the old man with the pompadour, who I now guessed was his grandfather. I wondered, should I apologize?

There was a pause in the singing as the piano player stopped to drink a demi in one long draught, and then the singing began in earnest again. The man with the pompadour stood up to sing. The children joined in, singing with gusto, though when the chorus came, I noticed that half the room seemed confused and sang different words than the singer had belted out. The song continued in this manner, and gradually people stopped until nobody in the bar was singing along, while the singer kept on going, his voice rising, and he swung his microphone toward his mouth as he came to each chorus. The mood in the room changed, and I noticed there was some murmuring at some tables, as if this song was unexpected, or this version of the song was abnormal.

We'd had a lot of beer very quickly, and I was disoriented and it took a few moments for me to posit what was happening. I had been watching the singer, and then I turned toward Matti and saw that he was standing, shouting something in broken French at the singer. The singer continued his song and—was he pointing at me?—nodded his head.

At Matti's continued protest, the piano player stopped and the room became silent.

I could tell that the focus in the room had shifted, from the singer to us, and I was embarrassed and confused. Matti now was shouting in German, which sounded to me harsh and strident after the rolling syllables of the French songs. He was a tall man, impressive in appearance and, I now discovered, frightening when he was angry.

"*Monsieur*," said the waiter who had been bringing us our beer. "*S'il vous plaît, ce n'est pas approprié.*"

I reached across the table and took Matti's shoulder. He shook my hand away and then began lecturing the waiter, also in German. I could sense that whatever initiative we might have had in this dispute, Matti had lost it by reverting to German, the language, historically, of the aggressor.

"This song, this is a song that is very against Jewish people," Matti said to me. "It is a bad song."

And he turned and in German began pointing toward the singer, who was smiling broadly.

I don't know why, but my response to the singer's pleased expression was to grin back. I didn't understand what had just transpired. I pulled at Matti's shoulder and told him we should go. What were we going to do, take on a room full of Belgian singers? On his way out, Matti knocked over his beer coming around our table, unintentionally pushing the table into me so that it made a noisy scrape and sent a sharp pain through my hip.

We emerged into the dazzling daylight, and I felt the weight of how buzzed I was. Instead of sobering me up, the confrontation had left me more befogged, so that as I chased after Matti, who was stalking down the narrow road ahead of me, I was still piecing together recent events. The escalation had been so sudden, the wind down equally rapid, that the whole affair, from Matti standing up and shouting to our exiting the bar, had only taken, perhaps, fifteen seconds.

"Wait, wait," I was telling Matti, who was walking ahead of me.

The streets were paved with cobblestones rubbed to a shine by centuries of footfalls. There were small dog turds on the street, little black cylinders the size of my fingers that had been covered with chicken feathers. Standing on both sides of the street, in the shadow of stingy lintels, were tired-looking women in long leather boots, short skirts, and sweaters. Black leather purses, old-fashioned, with a twist-snap at the top, hung from their shoulders. From the way they stood, their enduring glances at me as I walked, I gathered they were prostitutes. Liège's red-light district, I had previously thought, was similar to Amsterdam's in that prostitutes stood behind glass with red fluorescent tubes around them, but there were still some traditional street walkers here, I now saw, older women, perhaps aged out of the windows. I was distracted from catching up with Matti, who waited for me at the corner.

He shook his head, "David, I'm sorry. They are stupid."

I nodded. "It's OK. No, I mean it's not OK that they were like that, but it's OK that they—no, I mean, it is what it is."

Matti didn't understand me.

He shook his head. "David, are you hungry?"

I was, actually. My first encounter with overt anti-Semitism seeming to provoke in me a fierce appetite.

The restaurant Matti guided us to was down another narrow street and then halfway up a massive concrete staircase that climbed past little townhouses whose doorways opened onto narrow landings. We sat down at a round table in a corner of a close room with thick-paned, hand-blown glass windows and stone walls. We ordered oysters, terrine de chef, and suckling pig with red currant sauce—it was only after we had put in our orders that I noticed we had just requested perhaps the least kosher meal possible. Matti ordered for us a bottle of rosé from the Rhône Valley, which we quickly polished off before ordering another. The food was superb, among the best French meals I had ever had, and Matti regained his good spirits, talking to me, as he did when he was in a good mood, about automobiles. He told me he preferred the old Porsches, before 1995, because their engines were air-cooled, the simplicity of that appealed to the engineer in him, and he regretted having only one pre-1995 Porsche, and this a cabriolet, which he felt was too effeminate for a man to drive.

We were by now heavily intoxicated, the wine, the food, the low-ceilinged room all giving me a cloying sense of surfeit—I had ingested too much, the room was too small, the walls too close, the air too thick with smoke. The features on the faces of the local people were too pronounced. Matti had a capacious appetite, and because of his heavy accent when he spoke English, I couldn't tell if he was so drunk he was slurring his words or my own hearing was distorting what he was saying.

"What did they say?" I asked.

"Who?"

"The man in the bar. What did he sing?"

Matti said his English wasn't good enough to give me a thorough explanation, but that it was a very old song, from before the Second World War. He recalled it from his childhood. There were two versions, the first version was about Jewish women being promiscuous, and how you can have sex with them because their Jewish husbands are always working at money lending. That was the mild version. The more extreme version, which became popular during the war, which the singer had switched to after one verse, suggested that when you ran out of cobblestones, you could pave the streets with Jewish skulls.

This part of Belgium was very primitive, Matti told me, these are primitive people. Luik was a dirty city, full of primitive, dirty people. They were the only kinds of people who would sing a song like this. We ordered Bas-Armagnacs.

In my drunkenness, I kept telling him it was all right, it was all right.

I had no idea what time it was when we finally left the restaurant. We'd each had a coffee and then another brandy and more cigarettes and more brandy, and so the walk back down the steep stairs was precarious, each of us taking a breath at each landing, not because we were winded but to steady ourselves for the descent down the slippery steps. It had to have been late afternoon, but it seemed like evening. Thick, low-hanging clouds had drifted in, the gray, gaseous canopy so oppressive I felt I could leap up and touch the bottom of the sky.

Matti was walking ahead of me again, now humming something to himself as he walked, leaning over and steadying himself on the wall for an instant and turning to look at me and smiling.

How was he going to drive home?

I was also in no condition to drive.

We were on a curving road past a vast church with twin steeples. Over the entry to the gallery was an eye inside a pyramid, a symbol similar to the persiflage on the American dollar. There was a four-sided fountain with water streaming from the mouths of stone sculptures of male lions' heads, the tops of which had been rubbed so many times over the years the manes were worn down almost flat on top. They looked like they were afflicted by some sort of feline-pattern baldness.

Matti stopped and began sloshing water onto his face and then cupping his hands and drinking from the tap. Above him was a sign: *L'eau Non Potable*. He was already standing when I tapped him on the shoulder and pointed to the sign. His face was shining in a street lamp's dull light, the gray-brown hair on the sides and forehead of his face matted against his pinkish skin. He smiled and shook a cigarette from his pack.

He seemed indestructible to me.

I vomited near the fountain, rushing into an alley between a restaurant and what I recall as a furniture showroom. I remember being acutely embarrassed, both in front of Matti and at those strangers walking by who must have seen me, leaning with my head against the stone wall of the restaurant.

"Better?" Matti asked.

I shook my head. I straightened up but immediately reached for the wall to brace myself. I was no longer nauseous, but still I felt terrible. My head ached and I had that awful spinning sensation. I took care to move a few meters uphill from my own puke, sat down, and then closed my eyes for an instant but opened them again to fight off the spinning.

Matti was standing ramrod straight across the alley. He shook another cigarette from his pack and lit it with a match he struck across the stone wall. He inhaled, looked down at me, and nodded, as if my current state confirmed some opinion of me he had formed.

He walked away down the alley.

I was terribly thirsty and felt an urge to lie down on the cobblestones, when I heard shouting. Where the alley emptied into a more brightly lit square I saw two figures silhouetted. I rose unsteadily and went toward them.

Matti and the pompadoured fellow were squaring off against the base of a statue of a soldier in a kiwi-shaped, plumed helmet loading a musket—a monument, if I was reading the inscription correctly, to soldiers who had died in the Congo Free State in the service of King Leopold. They were shouting at each other, Matti in German and the pompadour in French. During a lull in their hollering, Matti stepped forward and launched a short right hand to other man's chest and they began scuffling. Their fight seemed slow and to lack energy, at least compared with the slugfests I was used to from popular entertainment.

A few spectators had stopped to watch, and there were children hooting—the kids from the bar, I realized. I stepped through them and into the brawl, trying to separate Matti and the pompadoured man, who caught me with a shot to my forehead that caused him to howl and grab his own hand.

Red flashing lights presaged the arrival of a police Peugeot, and suddenly there were two cops, one of them a short woman, and they pulled Matti and the pompadoured anti-Semite apart and then, to my surprise, placed only Matti in the police car.

"Why not him? I asked in French.

The policewoman turned and looked at the pompadoured anti-Semite. "Why?"

I wanted to tell her that he was singing anti-Semitic songs, but I couldn't find the words in French. "Where are you taking him?"

She gave me a card with a Liège address.

My clothes were stained and badly creased and my forehead bruised; I waited in the Jaguar as Lily-Anne walked up the proscenium-style stairway into the old, gray building to see about her father. She was gone nearly an hour. I tried to nap in the backseat but was kept awake by a dull headache. Finally, she emerged, pulling her jacket tight around her while her father, looking surprisingly dapper for a man who had been in a tussle and then the klink, trotted down the stairs after her, even managing a slight grin at me.

"David," he said as he climbed into the passenger seat, "we forgot the strawberries."

The wedding was an elaborate affair; the château was built atop the ruins of an old castle at the summit of a small-forested hill with a rolling lawn extending around the broken old walls to where the inner ward of the castle might have been. The couple's luck held, as the sky above us was eggshell blue, and as the guests strolled the lawn with their Pimm's cocktails and genièvre tonics, they did so in warm sunlight. Anna-Marie looked lovely, and I was keenly aware that compared with her husband, a dark-haired German with an Italian-sounding last name, I would make an unlikely in-law of Matti and Baumy.

Since our outing to Liège, I'd spent very little time with Matti, as the wedding preparations soon consumed even him. Lily-Anne was also busy, ferrying family members from the airport and train stations in Maastricht and Aachen to the various châteaus and hotels where they would be staying. Maison ClosDennis was full with family all the way to the rafters of the finished attic, and an additional chef was hired to cook for the forty-eight people staying in the house in the days preceding the wedding. The family's china sets were fully deployed, requiring the bringing up from the cellar of old and mismatched plates, bowls, and serving dishes. Keenly aware that I was lacking any clear role in this whole affair— the boyfriend of the sister of the bride is always a strange position; from seating to family pictures to wedding gift, my exact role and placement was complicated—I decided to help out one morning by bringing up these reinforcement dishes from the cellar. I had just set down my third tray full of dishes when I turned over a serving bowl with lions' heads for handles—I don't know why I turned it over, I'm not particularly interested in earthenware or china makes— and I saw something that surprised me: above the word and year *Altrohlau 1939* was a black line rendering of a modernist Imperial eagle clutching in its talons a wreath, inside of which was a big, fat Swastika. I began turning over other dishes and plates and saw more of this same marking. It was the first time I had ever seen swastikas in a nonhistoric or noncinematic setting, and at first, after I turned the dishes back over, I thought to myself that this was logical; I supposed that a German family would have a set of dishes from that period. They weren't the family's everyday settings, nor were they the fancy china. This stuff in the cellar was the third or fourth string crockery, seldom used or even looked at.

That night, the wedding's eve, in bed, I told Lily-Anne about the dishes, about the swastikas.

"They were my grandmother's," she said. "My father's mother."

"Was she a Nazi?" I asked.

Lily-Anne didn't say yes. What she said was, "I never liked her. She was a strange woman. She didn't speak to us very much. I loved my other grandmother, my mother's mother."

I said that I guess it all made a kind of sense, her father's strong reaction to the pompadoured singer, considering that he was also making up for his family history.

Lily-Anne put down her book and looked at me strangely. "What are you talking about?"

I told her about the singer, the anti-Semitic song, and her father's angry protest. Lily-Anne began laughing. "Is that what he told you? An anti-Semitic song?"

I nodded.

She shook her head and explained that he had bought an old sports car from that pompadoured man, a Lotus Elan Plus 2, which had turned out to be badly refurbished with mail-order kit parts. Matti had been fuming for a while about the situation, and finally, that day, after a few drinks, could contain his anger no longer. What I had seen was the rage of a cheated car buyer.

"There wasn't any anti-Semitic song?"

She shook her head again. "Of course not. Who sings anti-Semitic songs anymore?"

It was a rhetorical question, but I wanted to answer by asking her, "anymore?"

At the wedding, I followed Lily-Anne around as she greeted her cousins and the offspring of her father's various business associates. Matti and Baumy were each one of many siblings, and so the afternoon consisted of vast reunions of German cousins. Lily-Anne wore a silk harlequin dress over a tan slip and had had her coif done by the hairdresser in an extravagant up-do with some locks hanging down. Her sister had chosen the style for herself and her bridesmaids and it was fetching on Lily-Anne, accentuating her long neck and delicate ears. I admired her stately progress through her relatives, the ease with which she greeted family and friends. I took some pleasure in watching her among her family; they were such fine physical specimens. Yet when the sisters, brothers, Baumy, Matti, and assorted cousins and uncles congregated on the lawn next to the château, greeting each other with kisses on both cheeks, holding champagne flutes, smoking cigarettes, I would also feel a great distance from them. I was just a few feet from their blond hair, symmetrical features, and tall carriages, but still I felt very far away, from the family, but also from Lily-Anne.

But there was something else. As I watched Lily-Anne, she stopped seeming beautiful to me and more like, well, just another member of her tribe. I could barely tell her apart from her mother, her sister, even her father.

I soon fell back, as I again felt irrelevant to the proceedings.

The ceremony was a civil service in the great hall of the rented château, a vast columned room that opened out onto a balcony. A notary had come from their German ancestral village, and he read from a tall, thin, bound book as the groom and bride sat before him on high-backed chairs, holding hands. Before the ceremony, as the families were gathered, I had intentionally stayed out of sight behind a column, at the back of the hall, behind the rows of gathered relatives and friends, among those more distant associates who would not necessarily know who I was. Lily-Anne looked for me as the various siblings and their spouses were gathered and offered seats behind the betrothed. When he noticed the empty seat, Matti also began looking around for me. Then the time came for the ceremony. They turned toward the bride, and nobody noticed when I slipped out of the château and began my walk down the hill away from this family.

BARBARA HAMBY

Ode to the Messiah, Thai Horror Movies, and Everything I Can't Believe

When I decide to go to hear Handel's *Messiah* in London
        at the composer's parish church, my husband says
he'd rather see a Thai horror movie, so we plan to meet later
        at our favorite Moroccan lair that serves huge platters
of olives and fried goat brains, but here I am sitting in the pew
        next to the president of the Handel Society, who tells me
I've taken the seat of his wife, who has another engagement,
        and I see her sitting next to my husband watching
Shimabam Rampapoolajib rip the throat of a nubile virgin,
        then run through a seedy bar in Bangkok
and down an alleyway to the Chao Phraya River,
        much like the river of music flowing over me,
and the president of the Handel Society explains that in England
        they stand up for the Hallelujah chorus, and I assure him
we Yanks do too, and I think of the last time I heard this music
        I was with my mother in Honolulu and we both stood
as hundreds of voices soared over us like the gods exhaling
        a golden brew of divine moonshine, but here in London
the chorus is only twenty voices, like a group of friends whispering
        the secret to each other, and maybe I'm wrong
about the Thai movie, because I'm often wrong about almost everything,
        for example politics—I can't believe my mother
continues to vote against her own best interests because her father,
        dead over fifty years, voted that way, and why do people
have multiple sex partners because everyone knows about germs,
        not to mention staphylococcus, fungus, MRSA, nits
river blindness, and Ebola, and maybe the flying monsters
        over Bangkok are more moving than sitting in this church

where the great musician sat and listened to his glorious aria,
        "I know that my Redeemer liveth," and though I don't believe
those stories any more than I believe in Mothra over Tokyo, I do believe
        in the notes swimming over me like a river of fireflies
on a summer evening, and when the concert is over, I say goodbye
        to my new friend, who during the intermission
introduced me to all his friends, men in three-piece pinstriped suits
        and tidy haircuts, and I walk out into the December evening,
and if there isn't a flurry of snow, there should be, and I am so alone
        in this chilly night walking to the Oxford tube stop,
and I would love to see Satan bursting through the starry firmament,
        but there are no stars, only a stew of fog, and let's face it,
all our monsters are bivouacked in our chests like dyspeptic soldiers
        in a mercenary army, hungry, covered in warts
or contagion of some kind, too walleyed and stupid to see
        they are flesh and blood and there's a glorious song
somewhere inside waiting to be sung in a church or an opera house
        or even a pub where One-Eyed Walter is playing an accordion,
while a drunk warbles on a rusty flute, and Janet, the scullery maid,
        her sweet soprano like a tiny bird, fluttering out
of a corner so dark it might be mistaken for an entrance to Hell.

BARBARA HAMBY
Ode to the Triple

Valium, Librium, and Tylenol with codeine—that's what Velma
        the head nurse at the Florida House of Representatives
would dish out when you came in with your period, a hangover,
        a cold, a broken arm, a hangnail. She called it the Triple,
as in *It sounds like you need a Triple* or *That calls for a Triple.*
        God, the Triple was beautiful. You could do your job,
but instead of sitting at your squalid Bartleby desk
        and turning into a cockroach while proofreading
legislative bills commending beauty queens and putting potheads
        in prison, you would be floating on a cloud so silvery
that the words were a kind of neobeatnik dadaist poetry,
        and our goddess was Velma, a chunky bleached blonde,
who knew what was going on, so you couldn't show up every day,
        or even every week, unless you were a big-shot
representative from Palatka, say, or Steinhatchee or Miami Lakes
        in a sherbet-colored polyester leisure suit. O they could
go in any time they wanted and get a quadruple Triple,
        or so we in the proofreading pool fantasized,
because we needed a Triple to get from eight o'clock to lunch,
        when we were released from our cubicles
for sixty minutes, which seemed like sixty seconds, and Cindy
        used to say she wanted them to pay her every hour,
just pop the bills and change down on her desk
        so when she got fed up she could walk out with her cash
and never come back, and we couldn't imagine someone
        staying at a job so long they could retire, but Velma retired,
and the party was like an inauguration, because everyone
        who was anyone was there and plenty of nobodies too,
stiff flower arrangements, and a bowl of orange-juice-and-ginger-ale
        punch, and then she was gone like a dream,

and the new nurse was doling out plain Tylenol, which changed
       nothing, in fact made it worse, because when your head
or uterus calmed down, you'd go back to the trenches
       and wait to be blown apart by a German howitzer
or chewed by rats, so those of us who were able to escape
       might be forgiven for asking how it happened that one day
the door to that particular realm of hell opened and then closed
       behind us, much the way Burt Lancaster's hands gripped
Tony Curtis' in *Trapeze* when he did the triple somersault
       in the air or Babe Ruth's as he clenched the bat
and hit a home run with the bases loaded, but sometimes
       I find myself saying, "Velma, I need a Triple,"
and she comes down like a Caravaggio angel and pops them
       in my mouth and for a couple of hours I feel
as if I could do anything if only I knew what that could possibly be.

KERRY HARDIE

The Latvians Stir Ghosts

When I saw her in her urban kitchen—
thin and smart in her charity-shop green dress—
a glass wall was between us
polished spotless with some soft cloth of mistrust.
All winter she'd lived up the hill
in the gray house with the damp walls,
the rains fading the fields. The snow—
its ice-floe memories of Riga, darkness, home.

The nights we'd labored at her table—
those filled-in forms, the dictionary, the child's first homework.
Together, sounding out the words
that marched beside the pictures in his schoolbook.
The dog, dancing the leatherette sofa.
The baby, heaving herself slowly upright.
The bitter, amber taste of milkless tea.
All those months of friendship—now, nothing.

Was her warmth just a trick of survival
the child of an orphanage cannot unlearn?
Had my impulse been only my training
that no one should be so alone?
The house was old—others had strained before them
to keep the turf stacked and the children fed.
Awakening, had they heard this common language
and lent us grace to act a simpler truth?

December, with Antlers

Why are people wearing antlers in the hospital cafeteria?
—Because it's Christmas, silly.

Can't you hear the sleigh bells
drifting down like pesticide from all the hidden speakers?

Mr. Johansson says he doesn't get paid
                  enough to wear a Santa hat,
but everybody else just goes along with it.

It's winter, the elevators ding, the stunned relatives get off and on.
If it is Indiana or Ohio, they bring food.

No one sees the drama of the not-dead flowers,
taken from the room of the deceased
and thrown onto the trash.

Was it Stevens, or *Corinthians*?: "We make our dwelling
on the slope of a volcano."

You have to admire the ones who stand outside to smoke,
studying the parking lot,
all James-Dean casual with their IV poles.

If you could see them through my eyes, they all have antlers.
Human beings are tough, Jack—

with their obesity, their chemo, and their scars,
their courage in the face of dark prognosis.

Tough as Rudolf-fucking carcinoma.

Here come the three wise women,
up the escalator, bearing jello.

TONY HOAGLAND

Introduction to Matter

After I finally got over my sense of being a character in a book,

and the innocence had gradually drained out of me
                  through the holes life punctured in my container,

that's when I finally had time to stoop down

and look closely at the dry, exhausted-looking grass
                  next to the sidewalk, blowing back and forth all day,

and at the cracked, buckled plate of the sidewalk itself
                  pushed up from underneath by a live-oak root

and at a puddle of muddy water that had collected on the dirt driveway
                  exactly the color of chocolate milk.

After I understood that I was not going to be saved,
after I figured out that my imagination was actually not all that strong,

I took a walk around the neighborhood,

noticing the bottles overflowing my neighbor's garbage can
and the spatter of yellow flowers
                  on the unmown soccer field.

And, in fact,
after an intense, muddled, grudging, and prolonged intellectual effort,

I eventually grasped the fact—winter was over, it was spring.

In the high-school parking lot,
       the driver's education class
had set up bright orange cones,

which student drivers were weaving back and forth between:

practicing for a lifetime of going in circles,
         close calls,
not asking for directions,

and backing into things.

JOSHUA HOWES

Grace

It's been a month now she's been tutoring a dead girl on Park Avenue.

She says as much into her cell. She's walking fast to the subway so she won't be late—she has to take three trains. "We're doing vocab. *Great Expectations.*"

"What's that?" her mom says. "A blond girl? Does her hair color matter?"

"Not what I said," she says. "But I guess not."

"What?"

She can hear her mom talking to someone else in the background— it must be Linda. "Honey, I got to go," her mom says. "We're off to play the Porter sisters in doubles." Linda is her mother's fling, latest in a line of leathery-faced tennis-playing gym-instructor-type flings she's crashed through since the divorce. "Let me know if you need me to send money. I'd rather you ask me than you-know-who." You-know-who is already remarried, though it's only been a year, to a smooth-faced cello-playing ballet-instructor-type thing, an assistant administrative assistant almost exactly Grace's age. "OK, wish us luck! We're going to *crush* them. Bye!"

"Bye!" Mimicking Mom's chirpy signoff makes her want to hurl the phone at a passing bus, but then she really *would* have to ask for money. She used to get student loans, but since she quit the theater program she moved to New York for, she's scraped by on freelance tutoring and editing. You-know-who is disappointed, but it's not as if a theater degree, on top of the studio art degree she already has, would be any more likely to land her *gainful employment.* Those are you-know-who's two favorite words.

On the subway she finishes writing vocab cards. Chapters 14-15: *Obstinate. Disconsolate. Ironical.* In addition to definitions, she has to decide which ones Perry would get wrong. It can be a tricky business. Mrs. Bank is quite canny about which words her daughter would be likely to misremember. *Disconsolate* is difficult but doable:

Perry should recognize the root "console" and prefix "dis-" that negates it. This is one of the methods Grace has been "teaching" Perry. But "ob–" is a weird prefix ("against, in the way of"). *Obstinate* seems a good candidate to get wrong.

She arrives at the Banks' ten minutes early to find the front door open and the apartment empty. "Mrs. Bank?" she calls. She walks through the foyer. The living room is silent, expensive furniture glittering in sun. The doorman had told her Mrs. Bank was home. "Mrs. Bank?" This is *aberrant* (Ch. 5). It's *discomfiting* (Ch. 7). She looks into the master bedroom, where she's never been. On the colossal bed the dark-red color of a wound she counts the piled pillows (eight, nine, ten). She tiptoes to the marble bathroom. It's bigger than her studio and everything comes in twos: two sinks, mirrors, showerheads, what looks like two toilets until she realizes one is a bidet. She pads back through the apartment checking all the rooms until she's sure the place is definitely empty.

She's hurrying back to the elevator when she spots the utility door at the end of the hall propped open. She's never noticed it before. It leads to a metal stairway that ascends to the roof. Mrs. Bank is standing on the black tar past the water tower at the rim of a knee-high ledge with the wind blowing her blond-and-gray hair back and for a moment Grace is sure Mrs. Bank is about to jump.

"Mrs. Bank?"

When Mrs. Bank turns it's with a startled found-out expression and she holds her hand behind her back. Grace sees the cigarette smoke wisping out behind her and relaxes. Mrs. Bank says with a small laugh, "You caught me."

"I'm a little early," Grace says by way of apology, because it feels like she's violated some private ritual of mourning or healing or something else, she isn't sure.

"Richard doesn't know," Mrs. Bank says.

Mrs. Bank finishes her cigarette while Grace watches her mouth tightening with the puffs and the smoke carrying out above the city spread far below them, the yellow cabs banked like pellets between the avenues, the matchstick-little ceiling pipes and water towers and smokestacks of lower buildings, the wind blowing the tiny leafless trees on the sidewalks—it's all very pretty from this height because it's like a model, a toy, fixed in place for her delight, and she wants to jump with her arms spread wide and wrap it all into her.

Mrs. Bank flicks her cigarette off the building. "Richard wouldn't like it," she says, "even though he smokes cigars."

Together they go down to the apartment, where Mrs. Bank says, "So tell me about the essay on Ancient China; is it only supposed to cover Shi Huangdi or the Han Dynasty too?"

Grace has been tutoring—or "tutoring" as she describes it using air quotes to her friends—for the Banks since the day after New Year's. That was two months after Perry collapsed from what turned out to be congenital hypertrophic cardiomyopathy, passing out on the rubber floor of her building gym, with the treadmill still looping and thumping beside her as paramedics rushed in to pump her chest and blow helplessly into her lips. Mrs. Bank had described this scene in somber detail on the first afternoon Grace arrived in response to her ad on Craigslist, which had asked only for an all-subjects tutor for her 10th-grader. Grace and Mrs. Bank were having tea on the French settee and Italianate oak chair in the cold sun-dazzled parlor. When Perry collapsed, Mrs. Bank had been ten feet away on the elliptical.

"Perry wasn't a genius," Mrs. Bank had said at that first meeting. "I can admit it. I have my head screwed on straight unlike some of the mothers around here. But she worked very hard, and I'd say her academics were probably the main way we connected these last few years, so." Grace had sipped the excellent tea and watched the teacup rattling on the saucer in Mrs. Bank's hand. Mrs. Bank had then described the cutthroat school environment and which classes Perry did best in and which teachers liked Jews and which didn't and many other nonessential things that Grace had heard from a dozen other understimulated, overinvested private-school mothers whose children she'd tutored. What was different was that Mrs. Bank's child was dead, and Grace, uncomfortable with the strangely-lucid-yet-obviously-madwoman-in-the-attic-brand-of-crazy she was witnessing, listened politely with a frozen wide-eyed look and planned to make her escape at the earliest possible opening.

But for reasons she didn't understand then and didn't now, when

Mrs. Bank had asked, "Can I tell you more about Perry, Grace? Will you come into her room?"—was it the tea? it was truly excellent tea, a pale Darjeeling variety that Mrs. Bank called Himalaya Snowflake, whose taste Grace would describe as "austere"—for some reason, then, she'd followed the madwoman into the dead daughter's pastel-colored poster-covered bedroom, where together they'd looked at the photos, leafed through the journals, opened up the cabinets full of old dolls and toys, until two hours later Grace found herself in the shiny foyer murmuring, yes, she'd be back on Thursday, and, yes, cash or check, whatever Mrs. Bank preferred.

Mrs. Bank has given Grace the passwords to Perry's online school portal, so it's easy for her to follow the dropdown menus that list each class's topics and assignments. When she arrives at the Banks, she first spends twenty minutes reviewing with Mrs. Bank what each class has covered since the last session—what the English test emphasized, what the chem lab consisted of. They conduct this conversation in an abstract universe that does not contain the words "Perry" or "she" or "her"; instead they say things like "the World War I test was hard for everyone because it covered *all* Fourteen Points" or "conic sections will be a challenge because three dimensions aren't easy to draw on paper." After the confab, Grace disappears into Perry's bedroom for the remainder of the session. She checks off assignments in the dead girl's notebook, color-coding by subject according to the dead girl's system, and she makes cards with math formulas and history IDs and Spanish conjugations for the dead girl to "study" when she's gone. When the work is done, she usually has at least forty minutes to pass on Facebook or YouTube or e-mail, or simply to gaze out the window at the epic view of Midtown blinking in the falling dark and *hold infinity / in the palm of her hand* (they did Blake before Dickens in English). Sometimes she can hear Mrs. Bank turning the pages of a magazine in the living room or talking on the antique rotary in the foyer to her sister or starting to prepare dinner in the steel-draped kitchen, the sharp chunk of her chopping separated by as long as minutes. At the end of each session, Mrs. Bank puts the money directly into her hands and murmurs *Thank you, see you soon, bye,* and Grace rides the subway like a dragon across the waves back to the iron beach at Myrtle Avenue.

The day Grace finds Mrs. Bank on the roof, she tries to tell her friend Jules about it at his apartment. He's still in the theater program, an encyclopedia-smart director who's cofounded his own experimental theater company. He finds the situation at the Banks' alternately hilarious and depressing; last time they talked about it he cracked, "Next thing you know she'll be dressing you in Perry's clothes." He wants to know why she keeps going, and she says it's for the money, but lately she's been thinking it might be for something else, something more *abstruse* (Ch. 12: "difficult to understand, enigmatic"). Tonight Jules is distracted and doesn't see the point of Grace's story—what's the takeaway? he asks. She wasn't going to jump, right? Afterward they have halfhearted sex, and he goes back to annotating a new play while Grace sleeps in his bed. Her art and theater friends look down on people like the Banks, but Grace doesn't see why it's any more important that they put up a new version of Foreman's *Angelface* or get their old-timey folk-rock-emo produced than if Mr. Bank's consumer goods company sells people tackier pipe sealant or a gentler contact lens solution.

When she wakes up it's almost four in the afternoon. Lately she's been sleeping twelve, thirteen, fourteen hours at a stretch, but it never makes her any less tired. She's walking down Broadway to the J when she sees a pink pashmina shawl she recognizes bobbing toward her. The shawl is on the neck of a small woman carrying big Bloomingdale's bags who's talking to a taller similarly shawled woman carrying similar bags. There's no doubt the first woman is Mrs. Bank. There's a modest elegance to Mrs. Bank, a uniform of crisp light blouses, dark pants, expensive shawls (only the color changes) that's less Park Avenue than country home discreet. Grace almost bolts across the street, but it's too late when Mrs. Bank lets out a startled, "Grace!"

What follows is an awkward introduction in which Mrs. Bank says "Grace *used to be* Perry's tutor" and her friend puts on horrible sympathy faces that make Grace want to kick her ankles out from under her.

"So what brings you here?" says Mrs. Bank.

"I *live* around here," Grace says, surprising herself at the lie. "What brings *you* here?" she adds coldly, surprising herself again. But there's something about seeing Mrs. Bank downtown, especially out laughing with a friend, that bothers Grace, some kind of immunizing division between her uptown and downtown lives that Mrs. Bank's presence on Broadway and Prince has violated.

"Jane lives in Tribeca," Mrs. Bank says. "And she's been just *begging* me to get out of the house, so."

"Tribeca," Grace repeats.

"We have a wonderful loft," Jane adds helpfully. "My husband bought it *for a song* back in the '80s when the neighborhood was full of *syringes*."

"Also I was thinking of going to Chinatown," says Mrs. Bank, a frown crossing her face. "But I guess I forgot. I was going to get ingredients and try and make a pho. It's Vietnamese."

"I love pho," Grace says stupidly. That's not even true. She doesn't like Asian food generally, it's too spicy and mixed-together, which is strange because she's half-Chinese, but her mom was never much of a cook.

"It's pronounced *fah*," Jane chimes in.

"Right," says Grace. "*Fah*."

"Well, it's nice to run into you," Mrs. Bank says. "Be well."

At Grace's next session on Park Avenue, Mrs. Bank does something she hasn't done since the first session: she comes into Perry's bedroom. Grace is flipping through online photos of kids who stuck with the theater program when she senses she's not alone and pretends to be scribbling history cards. But when she casually turns a minute later, it's obvious Mrs. Bank isn't paying attention to what she's doing at the desk. Instead Mrs. Bank is sitting in Perry's pink armchair, the one that's usually colonized by old stuffed animals and American Girl dolls, looking out the window at Midtown.

"It was funny seeing you on a Saturday," Mrs. Bank says. "I almost feel like you don't exist independent of this house."

There's a pause.

"I'm sorry if that sounds offensive," Mrs. Bank adds.

"I understand," says Grace.

"You live near there?"

"My boyfriend does."

"That must be nice," Mrs. Bank says. "To be young and living in the city." Mrs. Bank picks up one of the American Girl dolls and looks at it with an unreadable—*abstruse* comes to Grace's mind again—expression.

There's a long silence, and Grace decides what Mrs. Bank looks like is tired, so worn to bits with carrying around her load of grief that it makes Grace want to throw her arms around her and dry her tears. But Grace doesn't move and Mrs. Bank isn't crying.

"It's a pretty view," Mrs. Bank says, turning again to the window. "I insisted we give her this room because it has the best view. You know we were in Westchester for eight years. I didn't want her to miss the sky."

Together they watch the last bits of red and purple being extinguished from the bottoms of the clouds, followed by the rough blaze of the streetlights coming on. When it's fully dark their reflections in the windows close the room back in on itself and they can't see anything outside. It reminds Grace of her old place near Ocean Beach in San Francisco with the fog galloping by the windows. She couldn't see the beach 99 percent of the time but she could hear the withdrawing waves. Sometimes she wishes she'd stayed there but other times she remembers why she didn't.

When it's definitely night, Mrs. Bank says, "It's past seven. You can go, you know."

Just then a timer goes off in the kitchen. Mrs. Bank startles up and pops out of the room. Grace is zipping up her bag when Mrs. Bank pops back in and says, "Or you could stay for dinner if you want. I made too much." Grace instinctively shakes her head. "You probably have places to be," Mrs. Bank says. Then Grace thinks about all the places she doesn't have to be and says, "I could stay."

What Grace hasn't counted on is Mr. Bank.

She's never actually met Mr. Bank, which Jules and her other friends say is weird but Grace knows isn't out of the ordinary at all—she's never met the dads of half the families she's tutored for.

She and Mrs. Bank are setting the table when Grace hears the key in the lock and a booming sitcom-y voice calls, "Honey, I'm home!" Men actually say that? she thinks. Her dad was usually more like "What's this fucking mess doing on the floor in the hallway?" Mr. Bank sweeps into the dining room already uncorking a bottle of red, jacket off, tie gone, shirt unbuttoned to mid-chest, and stops short at the sight of Grace.

"Hello," he says. He smiles bashfully and charmingly. "Ah. You must be the girl I'm paying a hundred bucks an hour to keep Rachel from jumping out a window. So far so good. Richard." He extends a hand and she shakes it.

"Her session ran late," Mrs. Bank says in a small voice. "And her parents live so far away. I thought it'd be nice to invite her to eat with us."

"By all means," Mr. Bank booms. "Why shouldn't a fake tutoring session for a fake student run late? What was it, fake vocabulary? Fake history cards? Balancing fake equations?"

He's still grinning cheerfully, which Grace finds much more frightening than if he weren't.

"This is how you want to act?" Mrs. Bank says.

Now Mr. Bank is clearly struggling to control his voice: "Rachel, we *talked* about this, I *don't think*—but now you're *throwing*—...am I right?"

Mrs. Bank just stares coldly at him.

"I should go," says Grace.

But Mrs. Bank says, "No, stay." She looks at Grace. "Please stay."

"Really it's OK. Thank you though."

Grace has taken two steps toward the living room when Mr. Bank's hand grabs her upper arm. He squeezes not very lightly.

"I think she asked you to stay."

Grace looks at Mr. Bank, and though the pressure on her arm is definitely not nice, there's something in his face that looks just like Mrs. Bank's and says to her *Please do I was wrong anything to keep it from being the two of us in this empty house I'm sorry.* At least that's how she reads it.

"OK," she says.

They all sit. Mr. Bank finishes uncorking the wine and booms,

"Well the food certainly doesn't smell fake, and this Côtes du Rhône had better be fucking *real*." He starts to pour Grace a glass. "I assume you're old enough to drink?"

"Twenty-five."

"Excellent. The peak of your powers."

He hands her a glass full to the rim. And suddenly he's all pink-cheeked joviality. Grace can't believe how fast his mood has shifted. For an hour he holds court over the table with delightful stories about his hapless junior colleagues, a disastrous trip to Bruges he once took with Mrs. Bank, a friend who wrestled alligators in Florida, popping open two more bottles of wine and laughing with a snort like a foghorn at his own jokes. At the end of the meal, he thanks her for being "a lovely captive audience." A few seconds after he leaves the room, she hears a doo-wop record come on in the living room.

In the foyer, Mrs. Bank apologizes for her husband. At first, Grace thinks she's referring to the standoff before dinner, but it's actually the rest of it, the part Grace enjoyed. "Richard thinks by pretending nothing's wrong, nothing more will go wrong. Except that one day I'm going to buy a gun and shoot him." Her voice is jokey but her face is drawn and pale. "Well, thank you, see you Thursday, bye."

Dinners with the Banks become a regular affair. This means Grace has to choke down pho not once but twice, since Mrs. Bank thinks she loves it and prepares it once in the Saigonese style and another time in Hanoiese. Mr. Bank is garrulous and booming. In photos, before she met him, she thought he looked like a dour, heavy-jowled person, but in the flesh, with his constant animation, he's handsome in a meaty, rich-guy, barrel-chested way. His head is shaved and he wears a little gold earring, which Grace finds out he got after Perry died. Grace can see why Mrs. Bank fell in love with him and also why she's not in love with him now. Between jokes and stories, Mr. Bank asks loads of questions, and when he's heard her answers, he says pointblank she's too smart to waste her time tutoring rich people's spoiled kids and he'll arrange an interview for her anytime. If not at his company then any number of others—he rattles off a list of titans he knows in just about every industry in the city, even sexy ones like fashion and music and publishing, which makes Grace wonder if all the superrich guys really do belong to a secret club or gather at a lair underground, like beneath the Harvard Club or Mayor Bloomberg's mansion, but then she figures it's just private school networks and who you meet at fundraisers. At one dinner, Mr. Bank asks to read Grace's palm—he says *of course it's bullshit* but he learned from a Romanian woman, *a real gypsy with three black moles on her chin*—and Grace looks uncertainly at Mrs. Bank who nods and Mr. Bank leans over her palm so closely his lips almost touch her skin and Grace feels an erotic charge pass between them. He says she's going to fall in love three times and live to be ninety and die surrounded by piles of money or grandkids but not both. She thinks she'd settle for fifty and falling in love, real reciprocated love, just once, but she can't really imagine either, especially not the twenty-five more years. She's already been hospitalized twice—once in San Francisco, where her room had a view of the Bay, and the first time during sophomore year of college in Michigan.

Later that evening Grace slips into the foyer to take a phone call from you-know-who (he rarely calls, which is why she answers, and it turns out to have been a pocket dial), and when she's coming back, she pauses for a moment in the living room, from where she can see the Banks sitting in the dining room in total silence. She's about to come back in when she overhears the following:

Mr. Bank (sudden, theatrical): "So one chicken was saying to the other chick—"

Mrs. Bank (interrupting wearily): "Stop it, Richard."

Mr. Bank (cheerful): "Fuck you, Rachel."

After that Grace never gets up from the dinner table again, not even to use the bathroom.

It's the beginning of May now and the school year will soon come to an end. Grace spends her weeknights drinking too much and sleeping until four with a compress on her forehead, which her therapist tells her *is not a healthy behavior* and which in turn makes her want to scream *OF COURSE IT'S NOT A HEALTHY BEHAVIOR YOU TWIT NOW GIVE ME MY GODDAM DRUGS AND DIE.* Instead they discuss coping strategies for avoiding alcohol, the first of which is to not have dinner with the Banks.

A week later, she and Mrs. Bank are bringing out an expensive cake that says *Happy Birthday Richard* with fifty-five candles packed into the frosting. There's been a lot of wine (so much for promises to her therapist) and after the cake they go into the living room, where Mr. Bank opens champagne and cranks up a Motown CD on the stereo. He and Mrs. Bank dance to songs like "I Heard It Through the Grapevine" and "Reach Out," but when "My Girl" comes on, Mrs. Bank sinks away from her husband like a tire slowly deflating and sits on the French settee holding her wine and cries. Grace doesn't understand why Mr. Bank doesn't cut the music, but then "Good Lovin'" comes on and Mrs. Bank gets back up with flushed cheeks and dances again. Soon she pulls Grace up with her. She and the Banks bop and shimmy holding their wine glasses. Grace does the twist with her hips flexing in and out and holds hands with both Mr. and Mrs. Bank and thinks this is the way family is meant to be. Then she remembers Perry with a clout of guilt like a slap of freezing water. Soon Mrs. Bank says she's tired and sits back down. Grace tries to sit too, but Mrs. Bank pushes her up, laughs, says *no, no, keep going, keep going.*

The tempo slows down when "A Whiter Shade of Pale" comes on. Mr. Bank pulls Grace close and puts a hand on her back. Grace glances at Mrs. Bank but she's half-asleep on the settee. It's not like slow dancing with boys her age, because she and Mr. Bank aren't mashed together; instead he keeps a firm grip on her back and maintains the span of a foot between them and leads her in an easy four-step pattern that includes an occasional twirl or dip. Grace realizes this is the first time she's ever really danced, like the kind of dancing they do on competitive TV shows and in historical movies.

When the song ends, she's surprised to hear Mrs. Bank softly clapping. Grace's face burns. Mrs. Bank rises unsteadily. "I'm done for," she says. "You two, stay. Good night."

Grace isn't sure this is a good idea. She watches Mrs. Bank wobbling toward the master bedroom. From the hall Mrs. Bank turns and looks back at Grace musingly—*abstruse* comes to her mind again—then Mrs. Bank turns again and is gone.

The next song is another slow one, "Tracks of My Tears." Mr. Bank steadies Grace's body and they dance as before. This is followed by

"What Becomes of the Brokenhearted," which is followed by "When a Man Loves a Woman." As they dance, their movement toward one another is almost imperceptible at first, but soon her body is pressed against his and she feels the heat rising off him. When he kisses her, she's not surprised and not not-surprised. They kiss until the song ends, and then he leads her by the hand through the hall past the kitchen to the little room the Banks call the maid's room, though nobody lives there anymore, which is the room farthest from the master bedroom. He lays her on the twin bed against the wall and his hands are on her breasts and pushing up her skirt. She's never slept with an older man; in fact, it's never occurred to her to try—she's only been with four guys, including Jules, who's not very good at it (he's jerky in bed and has a habit afterward of analyzing their sex, which makes her want to elbow his teeth into his mouth)—but Mr. Bank is very good at it or else she's just very turned on, which amounts to the same thing.

Above her his body is heavy, fleshy, dominating, like a man's body should be, she thinks, and his smell is different—musty, winey, somehow *older*. When he enters her, he groans with what sounds like immense gratitude. She wants to be pushed into, crushed into the bed, *annihilated,* and she whispers "*Fuck* me," which she's definitely never done before, and he complies until the bedsprings scream and they have to roll onto the floor. After he comes, he falls off her and lies on his back with his pants around his ankles, panting so hard she thinks he's going to have a heart attack. Wouldn't that be *apposite* (Ch. 36), she thinks and almost laughs. He gets up unsteadily and sits on the bed with his head in his hands. In the foyer, he gives her twenty bucks for a cab.

On the ride she's suddenly exhausted and thinks to herself dreamily *maybe I ought to be charging more than a hundred bucks an hour if I'm going to be fulfilling so many of the family's needs,* which feels like it ought to make her giggle but doesn't. To get all the way to Myrtle Avenue costs thirty-eight dollars and the cabbie screams at her when she only has thirty-four to give him.

When she returns to the Banks, it's like nothing ever happened. Only, when Mr. Bank is chomping away at dinner and tossing off story after story and laugh-snorting at his own jokes like a foghorn, she wants to throw a pot of boiling pho in his face. Not so much because they had sex—he didn't do anything she didn't do—but because she can see how his relentless cheeriness is just killing Mrs. Bank. The look on Mrs. Bank's face makes her want to curl up on the subway tracks. But it's different in Perry's bedroom. Before the dinners there's still the hour or so when Mrs. Bank comes in to sit with her on the chair covered by American Girl dolls. They hardly ever talk. Grace does vocab cards and geometry formulas, and Mrs. Bank knits or does Sudoku or a crossword, and usually by the end of the session they're both just looking at each other or else looking out the window, watching the evening fall.

It's the day after Memorial Day and in a week school will be over. Grace and Mrs. Bank are in Perry's room. Mr. Bank is away on business. Mrs. Bank has explained that she'll be joining him in East Hampton after Thursday's session, but she hopes the tutoring can continue when school starts again in the fall. Grace has said of course, but that leaves the empty summer and she's pretty sure the Banks' marriage isn't going to last that long. They watch the sky turning deeper shades of purple-red. A jet rises leaving a contrail of darker blue, like a sash against a dress. Grace waits and waits, as the colors slide down like paint wiped away by the cloth of night. It's got to be almost nine o'clock and she's waiting for Mrs. Bank to say it's time. She never wants to leave this room. Another moment passes. Then another. Then one more.

And that night she's at a party on a rooftop in Tribeca (she remembers Mrs. Bank's friend Jane when she spots a syringe lying on the sidewalk and thinks *Fuck you*). There's a live band playing, a brilliant moon hanging over the Hudson, a breeze coming off the river, everything you could want in a party. At the end of the night her friends are getting ready to go and voices are suddenly shouting her name. She's standing at the ledge of the rooftop, but not tonight, not yet. They all go down to the street and start walking. Someone says it's going to be an awesome summer.

BRENNA W. LEMIEUX
Precision

When I change lanes on I-70 North
toward the St. Louis airport, my father points
to my sideview mirrors and asks
how I like them angled. He tells me
he keeps his tilted to show only a trace
of his car, a shadow, enough to see
where it ends and the asphalt picks up.
And while he speaks, he leans his right palm
to show what he means and lines
with his left forefinger the wrist-hand seam
where his car peeks in.
      This type of precision
steers his whole life: gardens charted
to the inch, plates wiped clean with the heel
slice of bread, T-shirts tucked into careful
squares
   (*But I just folded those,* I say,
and he says they'll wrinkle in the drawer
like that); his paper napkins lie neat
after meals, evenly smeared with grease.

And when he hurries (at the airport,
say, late because his daughter got lost
watching his hands instead of street signs),
he wastes no motion: veers from the car,
seizes his suitcase, and skates through the crowd
as if weightless, as if his efficiency
could humble even gravity, could tempt
even time to turn around and look.

You Got to the Sea

for TP

The woman down the hall has a girlfriend.
When they fell in love the sea was a finger.
It pushed them both in the belly.
It rubbed their lips.
It ran itself up and down their thighs.
Then they got married. The sea came to the wedding
and ate the shrimp cocktail.
Had four martinis and danced its sea-ass off.
When it was toast time the sea got up and said,
What you want you can always have even if I drown you with my hot
     waves.
Someone broke a wine glass.
A bird flew into the window. It did not break its neck.
It shook off the slam, spread its wings, and took off.
Helluva thing, the sea said
and the two women kissed for a long time.
A year later one of them got sick.
The sea was nowhere to be found but in the sea.
It had other things to tend to. Boats and earthquakes. Things like that.
The ladies spent a lot of time on the floor in tears.
Sometimes they prayed. Sometimes they ate ice cream in bed.
Will I die? Will you die? Who gave us this horror?

The woman down the hall has a wife.
When you have a wife you pack up your couch.
You go to the hospital to get better.
If you don't go to the hospital
you go to the sea

even if it has abandoned you.

You put your couch on the beach and let the water roll up onto your
ankles.

You let your wife hold your hand and tell her to be quiet
when she tries to say nice things.

DAVE NIELSEN
Poem About a Still Life

A poem about "Still Life with Fruit,
Wine, Glasses, and a Bowl of Cherries," by Hendrik van Streek,
can't stay in the painting for long
unless it takes a closer look
at the blue bowl holding the cherries
and wonders, as the wall label wonders,
whether that's Chinese porcelain
shipped to Europe by the Dutch East India Company,
or tin-glazed earthenware
fired in the Dutch city of Delft;
but even then the poem feels antsy,
unless it leans in
toward the green napkin folded beneath the orange
and imagines a woman's lipstick
there, as well as on the lip
of the wine glass—half empty or half full?—
but again, even that's pushing it.

D. NURKSE

August on the Coast

The child imitating a dragonfly
zoomed into the dusty elms
and came back a child.

The child mocking a firefly
lit and went out
until he was invisible.

In honor of night
the child closed his eyes.

The child pretending to be a child
burned to grow old, soon he wept
in dry coughs. Always

the wind like a comb in your hair,
the laundry on its pegged line
trembling as if it knew you,

and the two named stars—
Altair and Arcturus—moving apart.

REESE OKYONG KWON
Victoria Falls Hotel

Even in this broken country, the women wanted to go shopping. The men arranged to have a guide from the hotel take their wives into town. The men were used to indulging the wives; the wives were used to being indulged; everyone was used to everyone else's behaving in agreement with generally held, old-country expectations. Wives shopped. Men arranged. Only Euna was acting erratically, and only at times. The others judged it understandable. Just think, they whispered, of her loss.

But all the wives were going into town, and for once, surprisingly enough, that included Euna. At the agreed-upon hour they gathered near the entrance to the hotel. *At* the entrance, they'd said, but they stood well inside the doors, enjoying the cool, gilded hush of the Victoria Falls Hotel while they still could. A very famous hotel, Jin kept telling them. A landmark of the British rule that prevailed here in Zimbabwe until the black people took their country back. Nothing bad could happen here. They nodded. They weren't reassured. All they had to do was look around to see the tarnish on the gilt.

Euna was last to show. As she approached the group, they saw that she walked too quickly and that she was flushed, disheveled, her eyes alive; the fall of black hair that made her look younger than her years was visibly unbrushed; she was, in short, so changed from her usual groomed and formal self that they cut off her apologies for being late with their curiosity. Was everything all right? Was she unwell? (They were all scared to death of catching malaria.) Had she fought with her husband?

Tactless as it was, that last question was the only one that made Euna flush again, so that even as the other wives disapproved of the inquiry, they were glad the questioner, Soyoung, had asked it— Soyoung, reliably the woman most likely to say what she was thinking. She had married up; decades later, it still showed. But Soyoung had to have hit the mark. What saint of a wife wouldn't fight with that Jin?

Over the past six days of their trip, each of their husbands eventually had confessed that it was Jin's fault that they were here, in Zimbabwe, where everyone was starving, when they could just as easily have been on the other side of the falls in Zambia, a better fed, less desperate place. But Jin was famously stubborn. The view, he maintained, would be superior in Zimbabwe. He refused to hear otherwise. The rest of the men had given in. For all her looks, Euna really was to be pitied. Anyone could tell that she'd been crying, poor thing.

So after the guide confirmed that all six wives were present, and as they set out from the hotel and into the waiting jeep, the women made sure to be sweet to Euna. They offered her sips of mineral water, they reminded her to put on her hat, her sunglasses. Their husbands were the old friends, having gone together to Seoul's best high school for boys, but after the years of reunion dinners in Los Angeles, the Koreatown karaoke nights, and now this first big trip together, the women could be companionable too. Their solicitousness would have confused Euna if she'd noticed. But she was flying. She was continents away. David was safe, and he wanted to talk to her. The open-top jeep bounced to a start, and they were off to the bazaar.

The car rattled down the road. "We arrive at the bazaar in five minutes," the guide called over his shoulder. And surely, Euna thought, there would be a payphone she could use while the others shopped.

"What happened to those streetlamps?" Soyoung said, peering over her side of the jeep. Pointing, she half-stood. The jeep hopped through a pothole—she yelped, grabbed the side of the car, laughed, and sat.

"Please! Madam, it is not safe to stand," the guide said. "I will tell you about the streetlamps but please sit down. This is because of the attack of the elephants last week." Everyone turned toward the destruction. Streetlamps, bent and snapped. A pair of telephone poles listed toward each other, crossing delicately near the tips. Like giraffes nuzzling, more than one woman thought, remembering the otherworldly creatures they had come from seeing in South Africa.

"Elephants?" Soyoung was patting her hat, adjusting the flop of its brim.

"Yes, Madam. They come into the town to look for food and they are very strong and some days they crash into the lights and the buildings. They are very naughty, the elephants."

"Do they attack humans?" Soyoung asked. Her camera clicked, its plastic snout lengthening.

"No, Madam," the guide said. "Almost never. When the people see the elephants, they warn everybody to go inside the houses. There is nothing to worry about, Madam, the hotel is very well protected. See, around the corner there is the bazaar."

One of the other women whispered in Soyoung's ear. Soyoung turned to the guide and asked, "Will there be African masks at the market?"

"Yes, Madam. There are many masks."

The woman who had enlisted Soyoung's help looked pleased, and sat back in her seat. "My son keeps a collection of masks from around the world in his dorm room, at Stanford," she said quickly, in Korean. "They must be cheap here, what with the currency problems, don't you think?"

She looked around for confirmation, and only then saw the others' stricken faces. "Oh, no," she said. "Mrs. Han, I'm so sorry. I didn't mean to—"

She fell off, lost. She had broken the moratorium—by implicit agreement, none of them had been talking about their children when they were around Euna. It was terrible. What did they have to talk about, if not their brilliant, beautiful children? But they had to be considerate. Euna's son was only six months dead: David Han, the model child, a Harvard graduate. Though they had no living relatives left in Korea, the Hans had gone from Los Angeles back to the old country to bury him. To return him to the ancestral land, Jin explained. To a woman, the wives had been polite: they expressed no surprise, though they knew Jin's background as intimately as they knew their own. His yangban family had lost everything in the war, and with only a widowed mother to help him, Jin had scrabbled his way back up to the top from nothing, just nothing. What land could he have? Either it was Euna's family land, or he was buying new land and calling it old. He certainly had the money. It was understandable. Men had to have their pride. Because of the distance, none of them attended the funeral, but from friends in Korea they heard that poor Euna had retreated to bed as soon as the ceremony was over. So broken by her grief, it was said, that she couldn't get back up to go to the reception. Jin stood straight-backed by himself in the center of the room, thanking everyone for having come. As far as they knew, she hadn't left her house until this trip. What could they possibly say to her?

But Euna was smiling at her, radiant. "Why is Mrs. Kim sorry?" she said. "There's nothing to be sorry about. Is Mrs. Kim's son studying history at Stanford? Anthropology?"

As she stumbled through an explanation, Euna kept a smile trained on her, encouraging her. It was all right. She knew what they were thinking. Yesterday, the comment would have knocked her down. But now she was airborne with hope. No one could touch her, and these women were fools. In a matter of minutes, she was going to be on the phone with her son.

"Yeobo didn't buy anything at the bazaar?" Jin asked, later that night. He was sitting on the edge of the bed, his jacket off, inspecting his shoes for scuffmarks. The hotel, old-fashioned, had requested that guests dress formally for dinner. Euna stood at the bathroom counter, smoothing foundation and sunscreen off her face. She could see the image of his image, the gilt bathroom mirror throwing back the dresser mirror's reflection of his bent head.

"No, nothing," she said. The bazaar—she hadn't noticed a thing. She needed a phone—she had to act like herself—she would slip out of the room while Jin slept. The guide hadn't been able to help her. There are many phones in the hotel, Madam, he'd said. With an effort, she added, "I did like the guide."

"The guide? What about him?"

"He told me a story," she said. She pulled snarls of hair from her brush. "About lions. He used to be a wild-park ranger, and once he took a group of Chinese tourists into the park. When they found the first lion of their safari, one of the women was so excited she lost her head and jumped out of the car, to take better pictures. At first, nothing happened. The lioness was sleeping. The guide was gesturing at her, but then the woman's husband liked the idea so much that he got out too." Euna stopped, realizing too late that this wasn't a story Jin was going to like. It had thrilled her. The couple's bravado, their devotion to the perfect shot. The lion's sudden, cunning spring. As she waited for the others to return, she'd pressed the guide for every detail. But she shouldn't have brought it up.

"Then what?"

Euna left the bathroom and sat by him. Her first impulse, to reach for his hand, was outdated. For six months, they hadn't touched each other. He'd tried; she shrank from him, each time; hurt, he stopped trying. "Well, then the lioness woke up. The guide said he thought she'd only been pretending to sleep. She attacked the husband. By the time they got a bullet in her, it was too late."

"What a disgusting story," he said, setting down his shoe, straightening up. He pushed out his jaw, its shovel shape. "What business did the guide have in telling my wife such a thing? I'm talking to the hotel manager. What's the guide's name?"

By the time she managed to calm him down—assuring him she hadn't been upset, pleading with him to lie down—she was exhausted. His predictability exhausted her. He didn't have to protect her. There was nothing left to protect. Not after the sham funeral he'd put on, pretending to bury their son. That she'd let him put on.

Euna lay awake and listened to him breathe. It was ten, then eleven, then twelve o'clock. Eight hours ahead—soon David would be awake, in the Sydney apartment she had never seen. Today, after lunch, there was the one, revelatory sentence in her e-mail, then the phone number, the black letters on the smudged computer screen a lifeline that David had thrown from Australia over the sea to Africa. *Umuni, call me.* It was the first time since the funeral that he'd responded to any of her e-mails that begged him to tell her how he was. Until today, she'd thought it possible, probable, that she would go to her grave never having heard from her first son again.

So much could happen over the phone. Seven, eight months ago: David on the phone with her and Jin, declaring that he was in love with some person named Alan. Another call, and David was announcing his intention to move to Sydney to be with his boyfriend. Jin: laughing, at first, because he thought it was a joke, then dismissing ("Gay," Jin said. "Even the word—foolish. As though life is all pleasure and you can run around doing whatever you want"), then cajoling

("This will pass. Trust Abuji. Abuji believes in you! You just need to pray"), then yelling ("You think you can spit on the family line? Once, we were yangban, we were aristocrats, our ancestors advised kings. Are you so selfish?"), then threatening ("You idiot, you should know there's a tradition of funerals that give up impossible children as being dead"), then his last threat. *Do this, and you are not our son.*

Then, when David moved to Sydney with his friend and Jin blamed him, a part of her thought her husband might be right. *Then* Jin said the shame was so great that there was no choice but to declare him dead, and he immediately made the arrangements: flying to Korea, explaining to the authorities that there was no body because his boy had died in a fishing accident, holding a funeral, going to Seoul's office of ancestral records, and striking David from the Han line, raising Jonathan to be the firstborn.

Jin murmured, threw an arm over Euna. She went stiff but it was all right, he was still asleep. For the next half hour, by centimeters at a time, she worked herself out from underneath her husband's weight. He clung to her, unconsciously shifting closer to her as she pulled away. But even as she fought him, she didn't entirely mind. In the quiet, like this, she almost forgave him. How could she not? She was as guilty as he was, which was also why the pardon never lasted. In the quiet, she still missed this: his nearness and his weight, his bigger arm holding her down. The first times they tried sleeping together again after David's birth, she'd pushed him away—their *baby* was in the room—and again the next time, until one night he'd gathered up her protesting hands in one of his and crossed them over her head, pinning her down. Soon enough, she'd stopped struggling; he was right, she was safe, and it was as though he'd taken away not only her freedom but also her shame.

At last, Euna eased her body out of the bed, brushed open the mosquito netting. He slept. Quickly, she changed into day clothes. In the bathroom, without turning on the light, she patted on a fast layer of powder. It was almost funny. Even at a time like this, her training held. She could fake her first son's funeral, but God forbid that she appear barefaced in public.

The outdoor walkway was poorly lit, though at least it was on the second floor. She shouldn't run. If anyone she knew saw her, there would be questions. An escaped elephant could reach this high, surely? The things she'd seen in South Africa: the red-jawed lions mawing their kill, rib bones the white of surrender curving through the mess of blood and fur. Nothing like running to excite a predator. As a little girl, she'd been terrified of the dark, and it was her father who conspired with her to make the dark familiar. He turned off the lights, taught her how to see. Feel for the walls, aegee-ah, he said. Listen. Trust your feet and make each step purposeful. Stalk like a lion, don't be afraid, pad down the corridor like the queen of the wild.

She crept purposefully down the long walkway, then she was inside again, and in the lobby. There was the phone, and she was alive.

"David-ah? David ihnee?" *David? Is this David?*

"Umuni, ahnyoung haseyeo." *Mother. Hello.*

"Where are you? Are you hurt?"

"I'm fine."

At first, his voice was slow with sleep, but already he'd shaken free, and she thought of the hundreds of times she'd woken him up because he needed more time to study: at five, four, three in the morning, she'd smoothed his forehead, whispered his name.

"David-ah," she said, her voice breaking. There was silence on the other end. He wasn't going to help her. She held the cold phone cord so tightly her knuckles jutted white from her hand, as if they meant to jump from her skin, wanting nothing more to do with her, and why would they? She knew how he was punishing her. Using the most elevated form of jondaemal to address her, calling her Umuni, not Umma: mother, not mom.

"David," she tried again. "Umma is so—"

"Yes, I know," he said. "Abuji tyrannizes over Umuni, it's nothing new. Umuni will have to excuse me for not having been in touch earlier. I admit, I was upset. I thought, hey, if my parents are going to bury me, I'll be dead to them. But Umuni kept e-mailing—why?"

"What do you mean, why?"

"Umuni and Abuji have already told everyone I'm dead." He paused, then said, "So why does Umuni keep e-mailing me?"

"We shouldn't have done it," she said. "It was a mistake." They'd stood around the empty casket like children holding a play funeral. She'd wept and people tried to console her until she couldn't stand it anymore, all these sympathizing idiots, and had to get away. "We should never have done it, David-ah." She was repeating herself. "How is, how is Alan?" she asked.

"Alan's fine." He sighed. "It's because of Alan that I'm calling. He's very close to his family here. He has a really, ah, happy family. We have dinner with them every week. Jonathan says Umuni's heartbroken."

"Jonathan says that?" she said, interrupting despite herself. Her younger son, furious at what they'd done, was hardly speaking to her and not at all to his father. "David, of course Umuni's heartbroken."

"So if Umuni thinks it was a mistake, then, well, Alan thinks it's no good, my being split from my family like this. Alan and I—maybe one day we'll get married. Maybe we'll adopt kids. In which case, I'll want grandparents for my kids. Does Umuni understand? I'm trying to be an adult about this. What if Umuni and Abuji say it was a—a mistake?"

"A mistake?"

"Just say it was a mistake. Say I hit my head and I was found in a village somewhere. I don't know. I know Abuji will be hard to convince, but this is ridiculous! Be my parents again. Otherwise…"

He didn't have to finish the sentence. He was his father's son. Otherwise, he wanted nothing to do with them. So she said she would help. She would talk to his father.

"How?"

"Umma will find a way," she said.

"Being gay, it's biological," he said. "It really is. Umma, we're born like this."

"Umma will help. Umma will find a way," she repeated, trying not to cry. He'd called her *Umma*.

"Fine," he said. Returning to his killingly formal diction, he thanked her, and if he didn't then ask why she hadn't been able to "find a way" to prevent his father from pronouncing him dead in the first place, it was because David was a good and generous boy, always had been.

Her first impulse had been to blame herself. As a little boy, David loved to watch her get ready to go out, peering open-mouthed at her as she sat at her dresser and changed her face. The delicate transformations awed him, the shimmering palettes strewn before her. He hid and unhid his eyes. He shouted with delight. "Umma is *beautiful*," he announced, and she conceded that it was so.

Too soon, David outgrew the desire to sit with her at her dresser, but when he came to her and Jin a few months after graduation with his declaration, her first thought was *Did I cause this?* At that point, she and Jin knew nothing about homosexuality. Living in their suburban enclave with emigrants like them, to whom did they speak but other, similarly misinformed Korean Americans? Jin worked with Korean Americans. They went to church with Korean Americans. All their news, from Korean newspapers. They thought homosexuality was another of the strange diseases contracted only by people who weren't Korean. Like obesity, say. Like laziness, like dyslexia.

"David-ah? Aegee-ah, are you eating well? Are you really all right?"

He laughed. "As my Abuji says: what doesn't kill me will only make me stronger."

After he hung up, she kept the plastic of the phone at her ear for another minute, unwilling to let the connection go. The handset had been cold when she first picked it up, but by now her body had warmed it and its touch comforted her, as if it were living too.

She was sitting in a narrow booth, glassed in for privacy. No one was at the reception desk, and the lobby was empty. A baboon paused as it traversed the edge of the floodlit courtyard. For a moment, it stared back at her, then it disappeared into the night. She had to get back to the room but she was crying, and what if she woke Jin up? So she waited for the tears to end. Soon enough, they would. She had become expert in the mechanics of her tears. The phone beeped in her ear. She flinched, set it back in its cradle, and got herself ready to go back to her husband.

For the next few days, the group took advantage of every available activity. They floated on a riverboat down the long Zambezi. They rode loose-flanked elephants. They visited a wilderness reserve and dandled golden, whimpering lion cubs. With rough pink tongues the babies licked their palms. The wives tripped over the dirt paths in high, hopeful heels. Euna, though, wore flats. Baboons swung lazily away. They were served afternoon tea on the verandah. The hotel was almost empty, a stage set for just them.

Guides accompanied them everywhere. Only the falls, adjoining the hotel grounds, could be explored unescorted. Giddy to be free of their keepers, they wandered the spray-soaked paths, they leaned on slick railings and dreamed. The air thickened with mist and ghosts. Water crashed down, each outsize gorge an act of God. Anything was possible, anything could disappear.

Camera shutters whirred, more insistent than mosquitoes. They were trying to cram the whole world into their cameras' mouths. They all took too many pictures, but everyone agreed Jin was the worst. He lined them up for elaborate, micromanaged poses; he braved the edges of unprotected precipices to get his shots. The others jollied him. (He was forgiven for having dragged them to this country, ever since the baby lions.) Did he mean to leave Euna a widow for the sake of a photograph? they asked, and he told them to smile.

Lightly, they discussed the country. It was shocking to them, the state of this place. Everything in ruins! Korea, too, a handful of decades ago, had been destitute, ravaged first by the Japanese, then by the Westerners' machinations. And now, look. It only took effort. Still, they were having a lovely time. In the years to come, as Zimbabwe, infamous for Mugabe's savageries, pushed its way into the headlines of even their Korean newspapers, they would remember how easily they had dismissed the place and shiver with pity, but for now they shook their heads.

As it got dark, they broke into couples and turned back to the hotel. Euna was on her best behavior these past few days, and she could feel how pleased Jin was with her. In a way, he was right. For months he'd urged her to get out of the house, and she said no. No to the business dinners, no to church outings. But it helped, after all, to pretend: the norms restored order. These people told a story, and she nodded, when appropriate. When jokes were told, she forced a laugh. She was falling apart, but the rules bound her so tightly they held her up.

Leaves shuddered overhead. "Jonathan would love it here, wouldn't Yeobo say?" she asked, at last.

He raised his eyes. "Yeobo's right," he said, and her heart pushed forward, but he was still talking. "We should take him on our next trip. What with the politics and the history here, there's a lot for him to learn. Maybe we should take our next vacation with just Yeobo and me, and Jonathan." His face opened into a smile as he looked at her, and his expression was so hopeful she almost told him everything. Hadn't he looked that way, courting her? Boyish and eager, back when everything was about to begin. They'd gotten to know each other in college, first as friends, then, more shyly, as boyfriend and girlfriend. Her father never quite trusted him ("It's not that he's poor. He's *pushy*. He's been denied too much, too long. That kind's never satisfied"), but when Euna was in her final days at university, her father fell down a flight of stairs and died. A year later, she married Jin. Now she was courting him.

"It's hard, having Jonathan live so far from us," she said.

"I know," he said. "All the way across the country at Vassar College." He did this. Anytime he brought up the name of Jonathan's school, he appended the gratuitous "college," as if to remind himself that it, too, and not just Harvard, was an institution of higher learning. Then he let out a sharp laugh. "But it's not as though Jonathan's even talking to us, right? Stubborn rascal."

Another day, then another. All the while, Euna was wild with thinking. David was right: wasn't Jin just going to say no? To have worked so hard only to have raised such a worthless, selfish son—this was what he believed.

One night, despite herself, Euna called David again. He asked if things were fixed. Not yet, she had to say. If there's news, Umuni can e-mail me, he said. He added, his voice so polite no one but his mother could have heard the underlying hurt: If Umuni calls me again, I'll have to change this number.

Then it was the last night of their vacation, and still she'd done nothing about her promise to her boy.

They sat by twos at small, exquisite tables. The seating arrangement was Soyoung's idea: sweetheart tables for the night, and the staff had obliged. A British family sat in a corner, but otherwise they were the only guests in the wide dining room. White silk curtains belled and collapsed. A host of white-jacketed waiters hovered like angels set to watch over them. It was rumored that elephants had broken into town again. A pianist and a violinist played a duet.

"Did Yeobo enjoy the trip?" Euna asked after the waiter took their order. From long habit, she avoided fowl. Jin hated the sight of poultry. As a boy, he'd learned to hunt birds in town streets to bring home to his widowed mother. She cried each time, at the disgrace, but it kept them from starving.

"Very much," he said. "Did Yeobo?"

It was a Schubert sonata, what the musicians were playing. For years, her sons had studied both instruments. "I keep thinking of the lion cubs," she said. She reached for his hand, and pressed it.

"Yeobo does like lions," he said. If he noticed that she'd reached for him for the first time in six months, he didn't say, but he wrapped his outermost fingers around hers. She knew the look and feel of his hands better than she knew her own, and they hadn't touched in so long that it was a homecoming. She pulled her hand away.

They ate bread rolls, then lush, filigreed salads, then springbok shank. Euna's steak came too rare, stained carcass red. Jin sent it back to be cooked more. She couldn't stop him, who could? The plucked flesh of flower petals lay strewn over the tablecloth. The music deepened from Schubert to Bach. More songs her sons had played. Hushed waiters made their plates disappear. Euna had no appetite, but she forced food down. ("Does Yeobo not like the food? I'll tell them to replace the shank with something else." "It's fine. I like it." "Is Yeobo sure?" "Really, it's fine.")

She watched him cut bleeding meat from bone, then dinner was over. Jin signed the bill, leaving a large gratuity. In general, he tipped well, but here, with the help, he was a bona fide big spender. "They're too thin," he grumbled. Waiters pushed apart their tables. For their last night, the hotel had organized a dance, a five-piece band. Chandeliers dimmed. At first slowly, then with more gusto, the couples danced. The beat quickened, then lazed. A woman was singing Ella Fitzgerald back to life. Jin led. Through her silk dress she could feel the heat of his hands.

They were dancing to a slow song, far from the others. "The hotel went to a lot of effort for us," Euna said, stupidly. She had no idea what she was going to say. Jin hadn't been born a hard man, no one was. The life he'd been given had tried to break him; it had failed, and he, Jin Han, had beaten it; therefore up with strength! Up with duty! Industry! Discipline! Willpower! Sacrifice! *What doesn't kill you will only make you stronger:* Jin had adopted as his own these Western proverbs, their unapologetic vigor. *If at first you don't succeed, try, try again. No pain, no gain.* When he whipped their sons for their boyish lapses, he genuinely believed it was for their own good. The half-dozen times he'd lost his temper and hit her—well, he'd been very sorry afterward: he'd clung to her and cried like a child, his tears wetting her face, and what could she do, what option did she have but to forgive him?

"I mean, it was a good choice, this hotel," she added. His face was touching hers as they swayed. She felt him nod, his jaw solid. What she never told her father: that she loved how pushy Jin was. She wanted his strength. And so, she'd gotten it.

"We're the best dancers on this floor," he said, pulling his head away to grin at her.

She tried to smile back. Then, finally, "I-talked-to-David-the-other-day."

His shoulder tensed under her hand—he refused to hear David's name. "Yeobo," she said. "Yeobo, we could say he's alive, that he was found. No one would think anything of it."

"What's Yeobo talking about?"

The songs switched, swung faster. "I read something the other day. It said that being gay really is biological. It's how people are born. Maybe it's true." She was pulling haphazardly from words she remembered David's having said. "Just think, what if we're wrong? Yeobo, we could all be a family again."

"Is this what David wants?"

"He wants his parents. Of course he wants his parents."

"Then he should have thought of how to be a son."

"But he loves his boyfriend. Just as we love each other. They love each other."

"Is he insane?" he said. He pulled away from her; his face was a fist. "It's impossible."

"But we could—"

"I'm not *talking about this anymore.*"

"Yeobo—" She stopped, trying to catch her breath.

"That seki. After we gave him everything."

"What if he never talks to us again?"

"Then let him go," he said, as when, six months earlier, she asked, in an effort to stop him: What if people find out David's alive?

Let them.

Jin said they had to dance until the end. So that no one would ask questions, he said. Three more songs, then it was over. She had trouble walking, but Jin kept his hand firm against the small of her back, steering her over the vacuumed plains of hotel carpet.

Once in their room, Jin sat on the bed and started to loosen his dress shoes. His posture was upright but slumped, as if he were hoisted by the back of his dinner jacket. Like the baby lions, lifted by the napes of their necks. His thin black laces slid apart.

She tried one more time. "Maybe something will, maybe Yeobo will have a change of mind—"

He looked up at her. The blunt lines of his face were softening, blurred by—tears, really? Here was the lost boy whose father had died in Pyongyang, leaving him at five years old to be the man of the house. "I don't know what to say," he said. "I don't know what to do. All I know is I'm not going to change my mind."

Her allegiance swung to him, crazily. She was the weakest woman who'd ever lived. He was impossible, but she was worse. With him, she couldn't trust herself. Already she could see clear to the day when she would once more start to see things his way. She would forgive him, again. She would reach for him, as she was reaching for him now, and it was only the heat and the press of his hands on her that gave her the idea for the one last thing she still could do.

The next morning, Soyoung was on the verandah with her husband having an early breakfast when she saw Jin and Euna setting out across the lawn. "The Hans!" she said. "Look, they're wearing rain ponchos. They must be going to the waterfalls. Why?" Before her husband could answer, she called Euna's name. The hatted figure paused, not turning, but Jin wheeled about. His wife followed him.

"Where to?" Soyoung said.

"I want another look at the falls," Jin said.

"Mr. Han and his pictures," Soyoung said. She glanced at her husband, who was chewing. "That's a fun idea, though. One last goodbye. Hey, maybe we should come along."

"I haven't finished my breakfast," her husband said. "I haven't even started."

"All right, never mind," she said. To be fair, she didn't want to skimp on her last meal here either. In the middle of their table, cracked rolls steamed. "Well, watch out for the elephants. I hear they're running loose again. How do these people *live,* you have to wonder."

Euna and Jin walked down the path toward the falls. This close to the gorges, the ground vibrated. From the first day of the trip, unlike the others, she'd worn flats, not heels. The other women thought her crazy, but she knew what she was doing. As though to prove her right, an unseen depression in the grass caught her shoe. She tripped, and Jin steadied her before she fell. "Here," he said, offering his arm.

She pretended not to see it. He was being especially solicitous. He had to know what this was doing to her, that he was killing her. So when she said she'd never seen the falls in the morning light and wouldn't it be nice to see, he'd immediately agreed.

They were deep in the mist again, the air soft. Vines dipped and veered green about their heads. The roar was growing. Ghosts of the children her sons once had been ran through the thick fog, pale sturdy calves flashing.

They stood at the edge of a drop. Across the ravine, a white mile of water sheeted down. Jin's arm was slung around her, the camera hanging from his neck. "A few last photos?" she said, and he lifted the camera and slipped off its lid. She stepped closer to the edge.

"Yeobo, look," she said, pointing. He came to her, the camera poised.

It should have been easy. The ground was slick, and he trusted her. She put a hand on his spine. She took a half-step back to position herself, but in the moment before she meant to push him off the precipice, she had the chance to look him over, one more time. His full hair, his firm, clean jaw. Every bit of him the man she loved.

Days before David was born, Jin had knelt before her. He put his head to her stomach and said that it was too bad, in a way, that the baby was coming. He hated that he was going to have less of her. She agreed entirely, but she stayed silent. Instead, she stroked his back. When his head shifted and he looked up at her, she lifted a finger to her lips and gestured at the mound of her belly. He nodded then, understanding. She didn't want the baby growing inside her to hear, not knowing then as she knew now that it was already too late, she'd made her choice.

Her husband turned his head and smiled at her. She couldn't do it. It was too late, the sacrifice too much. Half blind with tears, she snatched her hand back. She could think of something else—couldn't she? His arm closed around her, but she let him hold her up.

As she picked another plump roll from the basket, Soyoung caught sight of Jin and his wife coming back from the falls, their figures stiff, the gap between them wide enough to fit the child they'd lost. "Those Hans break my heart, they really do," she said, looking to her husband, but he was straining from his chair, flagging down a waiter. He didn't seem to hear her. With a sigh, she repeated herself.

My Ship Has Sails

Is poetry ruining my life, I wonder,
upstairs in a house with more windows than walls
where I am trying to write or read it.
Downstairs "Lady in the Dark," complete with dialogue,
too loud, and the purr of my husband's snore.
I feel a fume coming on, kindling
for an inferior rage that will not serve,
but ruins.
At dawn, before speech or motion,
a noisy crowd of hooded cowbirds pace
the perimeter. A woodpecker hammers
for delicacies hidden under tin.
The squirrel gnaws at the birdfeeder's cage.
I'm aswirl in words expecting something of me.

JANUARY GILL O'NEIL
The Blower of Leaves

Today I bow to the power of negative space,
the beauty of what's missing—the hard work

of yard work made harder without you,
while the stiff kiss of acorns puckers the ground.

I am a fool. Even as the red impatiens wither and brown,
they are still lovely. I feed the gaping mouths of lawn bags

with their remains. All this time I was waiting
for a heavy bough high above to crush us

but really I was waiting for you to say enough.
It was a feeling that swirled inside me,

a dark congruence, a tempest of the blood pulsing enough,
enough. How I had mistaken it for ordinary happiness.

I can forgive the wind rustling the aging oaks,
the clusters of leaf mush trapped along the fence line,

but with you there is no forgiveness.
Only refuse. Only the lawn's dying clover

and weeds masquerading as grass.
Nothing is ever easy or true,

except the leaves. They all fall.
Dependable as a season.

GRETCHEN E. HENDERSON
Unsaid

The auditorium falls to a hush. The audience settles in their seats. Sun backlights the room through a wall of windows: this evening of summer solstice. The first reader walks to the podium. She is a novelist, and this novelist smiles at the room, a graceful and warm and kind smile, welcoming everyone and introducing her project. She'll be reading from a novel-in-progress about a twenty-year-old girl, she says, and I listen as does everyone around me, still abuzz from the lively packed days behind and ahead of us at a literary festival nestled in the rolling hills of Ohio. In the back row, smiling, I'm sitting beside my husband and think: *a novel-in-progress, what a nice choice for a teacher*—to share unfinished work, to read publicly something rough around the edges—not sure if I could do the same without having figured out the rest of the story.

But before I can think about it more, she says a word. Amid other words: a particular word that halts my breath. My smile falls; my cheeks go slack, pale, less a color than the sense of blood drained from my face. *Doesn't matter,* I tell myself. *This has nothing to do with me.* But as she reads, my muscles say otherwise, stiffening in my seat, as I breathe my way around that word, and breathe again, thinking I've gotten the better of it, until she says something that makes me want her to stop. I'm not bothered anymore by that loaded word, which I've reduced to a comma, but by the character who is telling her story: that twenty-year-old girl who wants to be in a coma.

That's not possible, I think, almost shaking my head, tensing slowly, trying not to get angry. I barely shift in my seat. My husband turns to check on me, knowing this is not what I want to hear. The novelist keeps reading: flashing back to that twenty-year-old girl's seizure and an ambulance ride to the hospital with an EMT who eagerly asks if there was an aura. My mind goes on repeat: *There was no aura, there was no aura,* wanting the novelist to get the story right. *This is the wrong story,* I think. *This is not how it went. Because anyone who had been there would do all they possibly could to wake up that girl, if only they were able to reach in far enough to tell her she was asleep.*

My husband glances again to check on me, lays a hand on my knee, as I listen to this novel-in-progress that makes me feel, once again, that truth is stranger than fiction, which is why I tend to write fiction, trying to pull myself out of that novel-in-progress that continues to be read by that novelist on that sunny summer evening in the rolling hills of Ohio, but I'm back on a table in an ER in a small college town on the flat Illinois prairie, beside my husband's boyhood choir director because he is our closest friend here and my husband is out of town for work, and when I phone to ask that older man who has made music all his life if he can drive to my apartment before I get dizzier and more nauseous, if it isn't too much trouble, if he can drive me to a hospital, the last place I ever want to go and never do, if he can drive me there I will appreciate it, as I do appreciate it, as he stands beside my body, laid out on that ER table, starting to quake, not dystonic spasms that for years have twisted my body like a rag and taught me to learn adaptations and how to move all over again, not that, but full-out flouncing, no matter how hard I tell myself *don't do that,* no matter how hard I tell myself *this isn't happening,* no matter: as time itself spins out of whack, except for the thought that keeps scrolling rapidly through my head: *please do not let this be my last moment alive, please do not let this be my last moment alive, please do not*—before my brain short-circuits so rapidly that I can't even watch the words scramble, just go black, as they stay slack for a few days, until I awake from my comatose state and my eyes focus to notice, huddled around my hooked-up ICU bed, my husband, father, mother, and brother, flown from two coasts to the middle of that prairie, after two grand mal seizures seized a part of me that I haven't quite gotten back.

When the novelist finishes, I applaud with the rest of the audience, grateful when other readers' stories, essays, and poems invite me down their paths of pathos into humor that makes me laugh aloud, displacing that pit in my stomach and held breath, brightening my cheeks, drying my eyes, making that Illinois ER recede away on the prairie. My husband holds my hand. It isn't a story I tell people, because I do not want to be branded: *that girl who almost died.* Time and distance make her recede farther from me, so that thirty-three-year-old girl who woke in the middle of winter and found her words didn't make sense, who worked her wobbly legs around the ICU again and again and again (first held up by two bodies, then one, then holding up herself), that girl who slowly studied crosswords and read aloud her prior writings until words made sense again, that girl who went back to teach part time a week after she awoke, because she didn't want her health to ever get the better of her (even as it did), that girl: I've wished was fiction but know that she is me.

And after the reading on the night of the summer solstice—knowing that the novelist who read is a talented and thoughtful writer, knowing that everyone has the right to tell any story, knowing that every story about the same thing is different as much as our bodies are—after that reading, at a bookstore signing, I pass by that novelist who wrote of the girl and her seizures and coma and want to tell her *I was there and can't imagine her not wanting to come back,* but only manage to say *That was a lovely reading,* and thanked her for her words.

GRETCHEN PRIMACK
You Are a Prince

You are a wretch and a leech and a dirty
old man and have been trying to push
inside me for years. Well, come on then.
There's something about the plum warm

air. Usually at this time of day I don't
want to see people. Usually when I'm on
the old swings I think about the man
who stopped his car here and asked me
how to get somewhere and he was naked.
So what. I walked back to the swings
and he drove off with his dumb worm

and his hatchback. That was years ago
and now the seeds are tired of assembling
grass in all this seediness. Come on then.

GRACE SCHAUER
Wake

for my mother, Veronica Cazier (1955-1991)

The undertaker gripped my hand. I said I wanted Dairy Queen.

I touched her cheek because I needed proof—and after, Dairy Queen.

It's what I asked for every day: to go to Dairy Queen.

Worse than dead, she wasn't quite herself. I pictured Dairy Queen.

I'd finished second grade and hadn't been to Dairy Queen.

I can't recall who asked, or why. I know I brought up Dairy Queen.

When she drove me home from school we'd always pass the Dairy Queen.

She wore her wedding dress. Her lips were lipstick red, then blue.

My uncle waited just outside. I left, still wanting Dairy Queen.

MARIA TERRONE

A Hologram State of Mind

That glass of wine suspended in air
decades ago—3D projection still a tactile
memory, the ruby liquid shimmering
as if just poured into its goblet,
the hands reaching out,
all of us incredulous then believing
before this chalice raised to science and art.

And now in Japan, rising pop diva
cat girl Hatsune Miku—high-def,
green-haired avatar—"sings"
synthesized pop in huge stadiums,
bloodless and breathless
for thousands of fans.

Today as the self-described
"philosopher of blogging" lectured,
the word "virtual"
crawled off the PowerPoint screen
over his skin, and I wondered
if he knew what we saw
and what we believed was true.

Telemetry

On a good day, surgery lasts three minutes or less. Today's takes longer. Kathryn has an audience.

They don't touch the fish at this point—they try to handle them as little as possible—but for the girl, Kathryn makes an exception. She wets her hand in a clear plastic bucket and lifts the stunned fish from the net. A wild brook trout, with a beating heart no bigger than a ruby. The girl leans in to wonder at the gently heaving side, the cool vermiculated skin. It comes to life and squirms in Kathryn's hand. She grips down—gentle, but firm. The girl squeals a little. She can't be more than seven. She has the kind of light blond hair that darkens with age. In ten years she'll pick up a picture of herself and see a stranger.

"Wet your hand," Kathryn says.

Kathryn has to stop thinking of her as *the girl.* Her name is Shelly. Kathryn's never been able to see children as real people. She wonders what this says about her. Shelly puts a tentative finger to an adipose fin, a sleek belly, a black mouth.

In Kathryn's first summer on Back Allegheny Mountain, the trout and the bright scalpel made her squeamish. Fear of killing something so delicate, so rare. Two years later, the work is rote. She has to remind herself that the place is beautiful: a rich pelt of red spruce, wildflowers, and pools of glacial blue, each set like a sapphire in the spiky ring of a beaver dam. She doesn't notice the sweet balsam on the wind, or the river smell, equal parts iron and moss. The odd bear will wander through camp and savage a cooler, reminding her what the mountain still is. The Monongahela National Forest begins a mile downstream. A ski resort owns this land, ten thousand acres. So far, they have left this part undeveloped—or *underdeveloped,* as the Chamber of Commerce says.

"You better toss him in."

A male voice behind them. Gary, bossy as always, is standing knee-deep in the Shavers Fork of the Cheat River. It laps at crudely patched neoprene waders. Lifting the electroshocking wand high overhead, he reaches a free hand down to the river. He takes a palmful of water and rubs it over his face. Water droplets gather in a patchy beard, each a prism.

"By the book, by the book," he crows. "What would the University Animal Care and Use Committee say? Ain't you a member of said committee?"

Kathryn rolls her eyes. Shelly smiles at that. Kathryn dumps the trout into another plastic bucket, cold creek water dosed with a clove oil solution. An anesthetic and antiseptic. Shock, drug, cut. A wonder it doesn't kill them. The trout swims in a lovely sinuous line, resting on nervous fins. Sleek skin the color of mint and coal fire. The trout lists to its side, loses equilibrium, and floats to the surface. Kathryn scoops it up.

Her scalpel licks its side, below the ventral line. A clean incision, millimeters.

"Give it here."

She takes the telemetry device from Shelly's palm. A mechanized pill, clear and crammed with minute machinery, with a fiber optic tail. It recalls the sterility of good hospitals, all mankind can accomplish. Kathryn slides it into the incision. Shelly winces.

"Don't worry. He can't feel a thing."

"Fish don't hurt?"

"No. Not that. He's just sleepy."

Initially the trout drove her crazy. The movements seemed erratic. Had the telemeters malfunctioned? Did the new cellphone tower throw them off? Kathryn had icepick headaches and spent a lot of time in her sleeping bag. Patterns then emerged. To say the least, this population is mobile. Maybe the highest rates ever recorded in the mountain chain. Besides the odd flutter of anxiety, she is confident in the numbers.

Kathryn whip-stitches three sutures to close the incision, eases the trout into a bucket of plain river water. As they wait for the clove oil to wear off, she explains their research to Shelly, how they track the movement of brook trout between the mainstream and the tiny tributaries. How far do they go? Do they migrate because of rising water temperatures? Is there an identifiable trigger? That's her hypothesis.

"If you come back tomorrow, I'll show you how. We use a radio transmitter. It's fun. It's like on the movies."

"Thanks for showing me, Kathy."

"Kathryn. It's Kathryn." She smiles at the girl quickly, ferociously—a bad habit of hers.

Shelly blushes, runs off in a gawky clatter of limbs. Dumbfounded, Kathryn watches her go. Grasshoppers fling themselves out of her path. One hits the river. A trout snaps it up.

Gary says, "Strike another blow for women in the sciences."

Kathryn laughs, a good sport, though she's disappointed. She wanted to plug a laptop into the generator and show off her program: those wandering lavender dots, x-axis and y-.

The trout has righted itself. After taking measurements on a digital scale, Kathryn walks it to the water and works it back and forth in the current. Number thirty. Gills flare. In a realization she can almost feel, the trout kicks off in a little starburst of relief. The trout's lie is no bigger than a bathtub. She lifts her tickled palm.

Gary wades out and unhitches his pack, dainty for a big man. He respects the equipment. They drive back to camp in her big bouncing Ford. It parts the field like a frigate. The other member of their team, Michael, the one Kathryn is sleeping with, is still asleep in her tent.

That afternoon, the girl begins stealing. Michael notices first. He finds plastic tubs open, ones they are fastidious about closing. Nothing expensive, a bag of dried apples, a warm bottle of beer. The next day, a flathead screwdriver. At first they think it's the girl's father. They don't know his name. Why not a shotgun, why not the GPS?

And Michael says, "Of course it's the kid. She walks past a laptop for cereal."

"Shelly?"

Gary gawps at them. He says, "You've got a double agent on your hands."

They glance over at the only other camp, a good hundred yards off. Muddy blue jeans strung on a line. A resiny ax wedged in a hemlock. The pup tent is bedraggled, decades old. A sharp contrast to the researchers'. Kathryn's truck is solid with gear. Enough to invade a small Arab nation, Michael says. This makes her feel bloated. Those bins packed solid with food, electronics, clothes. A glut of technology. Who needs all this shit?

Ever since the pair showed up three days ago, the researchers have sensed something was off. First, a man near thirty and a little girl alone—you assume the worst, no matter how unfair that is. They don't wear hiking boots, but tennis shoes. They don't have a good way to cook their food, just a fire ring. They are poor. They never came to say hello–the researchers are desperate for new voices, new faces. Kathryn finally caught the girl watching them and coaxed her over. Her dad has a bruised look around his eyes. At night they hear him talking to himself, or to Shelly, except some nights he does not. He has an army surplus pack, Korea vintage.

It's near four when the team makes dinner. They're too disturbed to focus. Gary says, "I'm marching over there and asking them to lend me my screwdriver. I need it."

"'Marching over there'?" Michael says. "Leave it alone. They don't have shit."

"I'm pissed. I buy good tools. The best. *Consumer Reports* and everything."

Kathryn says, "Just let it go. Don't be the world's youngest fussy old man."

As soon as she says that, Gary softens, cools, is as bland as candlewax. She hates that about him. They spent the first summer here alone, having a grand old time until he drunkenly propositioned her. He was only half joking. She laughed at him. She still regrets that. He stalked off to his tent, and they never discussed it. Michael joined the second year, after his own work fell apart like so much wet cardboard. (He's now exploring the effects of woody debris on trout habitat, a topic Gary calls flimsy.) Michael was studying strip-mining effects on the next watershed, till he gave a bitter, truthful interview to a newspaper. Consol Coal banned him from its property. Turns out he was sneaking through a hole in the fence, for which he still faces trespassing charges. They have chilling surveillance video of him taking water samples. The department chair bailed Michael out of the Upshur County jail. The chair couldn't have been more proud.

He asked Kathryn to make room. She invited Michael on before she realized, far too late, that Gary hated him with the dull white fury of an acetylene torch. Both are younger than Kathryn, just master's students. Michael is inspired, combative, a sloppy researcher—everything work-manlike Gary is not. Michael is handsome, everyone's favorite. Gary, soft and baggy, is tolerated. Worse, the spite isn't mutual.

Kathryn says, "I'll buy you a new screwdriver."

"Don't patronize me, K."

"I'll let you chop onions," she says with her sweetest smile.

"'The woman said.'"

"Fuck you."

She says it with cheer. Since the president of Harvard made his comments, they have been paying ironic tribute to Kathryn's role as "woman scientist." Michael fixes on them the cockeyed, pedantic look of a deranged professor. He says, "Domesticity suggests peace. All sociology tells us so. It is the realm of the calmer emotions."

Michael seems more charming than he actually is, when she actually grits down and listens to the things he says. She wonders if this is a tic of evolution—that easy flashing smile, meant to attract her, distract her, like a crow to aluminum foil. The easing of standards.

Cooking does calm them. Michael leaves to filter water. Gary handles knives. Kathryn primes the portable stove and cups a lit match against the wind, bearing it like an acolyte.

She didn't plan on sleeping with Michael, not up here, not ever. A way to pass the time, she notes glumly. He lives with a girlfriend in Morgantown, a nice third-grade teacher with a flapper haircut, prettier than her. *But who isn't nice?* Kathryn muses. *We're all nice. Nice, nice, nice.* He's six or seven years younger than Kathryn—that's what stings. It feels so cheap, so glitter-and-trash. She should feel worse about the girlfriend.

Across the field, the man dumps armfuls of branches into the fire ring, then pours kerosene on them. Their dinner will consist of cans. Maybe they have nowhere else to go.

Shelly steps out of the tent. She's been sleeping. She waves at Kathryn. Kathryn doesn't know what to do, except wave back. The man does too.

"All hail the good thief," Gary says as he whets the knife.

After dinner, Gary scours their pots with sand. When he gets back he says, "I want to shoot some guns."

"I'm not in the mood," Kathryn says.

"I'm in the mood."

"It's OK," Michael says to Kathryn. "You don't want to bother them, do you?"

"I don't like kids and guns in the same space."

"I'll go talk to them. I'll ask if it's OK."

Gary says, "I don't give a damn. I hauled three gross clay pigeons up here and we are going to shoot every one. We are going to drink beer and we are going to shoot guns. It's Friday night and we are Americans."

"Easy. Five minutes."

As Michael crosses the field, Kathryn packs away the stove. Gary goes round to the far side of the truck, where she can't see him, and sifts through boxes. He slides a double-barrel twelve-gauge out of a soft case and cracks it open. The metal sounds crisp.

It's a safe place to shoot. They camp in "the field," the timber ghost town of Spruce. Nothing's left but scorched foundations, a lone switch-man's shack, and the odd pile of rusted peavey heads in the weeds. At four thousand feet, Spruce was once the highest incorporated town in the east. Fifteen hundred people lived up here—with hotel, church, and post office—but they never buried anyone, the true measure of settlement. Spruce lasted twelve years. It's an old story, no secret place. In spring and fall, fishermen bound for Shavers walk seven miles up the ruined track. Kathryn has finagled a gate key to the private road—she's the only native in the department and knows how to talk—and fishermen are amazed to find a big dual-wheeled truck parked up there. "How'd you get on that road?" they ask, salivating. "Connections," she says. In bright summer, trout grow wary and fishermen leave. The researchers have it to themselves. Until that man and his girl appeared.

Birds shatter from the field.

He shot me.

He didn't, no, he shot a beer bottle on a stump. Battering off the ridge, echoes recede in waves. Gary pops open the breach and twin trails of gunsmoke drift. Kathryn has to sit. She pats herself down. She clutches her head, as if to keep it from being unscrewed.

"Sorry! K., look at me. I didn't mean to scare you. I thought you saw me. I did."

Michael returns with man and daughter in tow. Shelly says to Kathryn, "I know you!"

The man sticks out his hand. "I'm Russ," he says. "Russ Nedermeyer. Good meeting you."

Names and bottles of beer are introduced all around. Nedermeyer keeps on talking. He has an Eisenhower jacket, a brown crew cut under a ball cap, and a five-day beard—in an odd way, he looks clean-shaven just the same. It's his stride, crisp and confident, and he wears a camouflage T-shirt, the kind sporting-goods stores sell from a cardboard box. It sags over a slight belly and blue jeans gone white and soft. Kathryn can tell he's local. He has that accent, somewhere between a twang and a brogue, a run-on voice with words tripping over each other and along. Not southern, but musical and watery, like stones knocking underwater. An accent Kathryn has taken pains to cull from her own throat. She wants to be taken seriously.

Gary says, "You all are on vacation up here."

It's not a question.

Nedermeyer grins. "That's right. Shelly and me are having a big time."

"You like to shoot?"

"Love it."

Everyone makes sure to keep Shelly back, and she revels in the attention. They sink each leg of the clay-pigeon thrower and point it at the forest. The string has dry-rotted, so Gary's bootlace is volunteered. Discs are flung in wild wobbling arcs, slivers of toxic orange against the blue. They shoot for an hour. Shoulders purple and ache sweetly. Nedermeyer cancels one and cancels the other. He can't miss. He knocks double after double from the sky, the best shot by far.

"I was a piss-poor till the navy. You'd be surprised how much the navy makes you shoot. You wouldn't think that, would you? Maybe we ought to bet money on this. No?"

Between shots, he delivers a running monologue on their family life. Some of it makes Kathryn blush, with Shelly there listening. He says, "Her mom's on drugs. She's living in Baltimore. It's a damned crack house. She don't even get visitation. Wish I was lying to you."

That's hard, they all agree.

Nedermeyer makes a little shrugging hitch with his shoulders. "Her decision," he says. "Last time I went, there had to be eight guys in there, smoking the pinkest biker rock you ever seen. Air tasted like Drano on the back of your tongue. Don't marry young, is all I can say. I got Shelly out of there. Judge drug his feet on it like you wouldn't believe. No telling what she saw."

Separately, the adults imagine the vile things Shelly has seen.

Readjusting to this, Kathryn looks at the girl. No response. She's heard all this before. Yellow piles of shotgun hulls accrue at their feet, and Shelly makes a game of racing forward between shots and gathering them up. Nedermeyer hands the shotgun over to Kathryn. "Knock them down," he says. "Shelly! Get back from there! Throw-arm on that thing break your effing leg."

Kathryn shoots a dozen times, missing all but three. She's distracted.

"You lost your touch," Michael tells her.

"Comes and it goes," she says and hands the shotgun back.

Gary drinks beer and makes small talk with the girl. He's good with children. It's surprising. Kathryn feels a little off-balance. Maybe she's drinking hers too fast.

Nedermeyer tells them, "God, I love this. Been too long. Too long. We used to hunt grouse. Raised English setters. My dad, I mean. No more birds to speak of. Pull."

Kathryn smiles in spite of herself. Nedermeyer is half the people she went to high school with: a garrulous semi-conman, damn good with tools, maybe a little into drugs, basically harmless. A serious talker. He's a new type for the others. They spent their years in the labs and classrooms of a tamed college town. They don't know the local animals. Gary's from the suburbs of Minneapolis, and Michael grew up in D.C., the only white kid in his school.

It's inevitable, so Kathryn asks Nedermeyer where he's from.

They grew up a few miles apart, in Tuscarora County, to the north.

"What's your last name?" he asks.

"Tennant," she says.

"I know your dad." Then, more softly: "Well, I knew him."

Kathryn's heart thrills and saddens at the same time. Nedermeyer doesn't say anything else. He senses not to. She sees that in his face. He offers the box of shells and she waves it off.

Gunpowder curling in her nose. It reminds her of squirrel hunting with her father. No one thought it strange, he had no sons. Her mother would boil two eggs in the dark kitchen, and Kathryn would stick her hands in the pockets of the oversize hunting vest and clutch them for warmth. Once they cooled, she'd peel each egg in the woods for a late breakfast. Her father smiled as she popped each yolk, a miniature sun, into her mouth. Before each shot he'd whisper, *Plug your ears.* Sitting on a log with him, she could feel the dull muffled percussion though her seat, her spine. Bodies fell from the trees. Gathering them into the game bag in her vest. Feeling them lose warmth against her back. Soothing, and strange.

Nedermeyer closes the shotgun with a muted thunk. "Nice piece," he says to Gary. "I like this gun. I like a 26-inch barrel. Nice and quick. Whippy. A bird gun. It's choked improved cylinder and modified? Classic. No sense changing it." He makes a show of looking at the barrel, reading embossed letters. He says, "I never heard of Ithaca before. That a new make?"

"No. The Japanese make it."

Nedermeyer slaps his head and makes a goggle-eyed funny face. His daughter laughs. Kathryn suddenly loves the man.

Nedermeyer looks around. "The mountains," he says. "Love it up here. Love it! Even in July. Couldn't live nowhere else. I'm done moving around."

They take in the ridgeline, the blue dusk. In the distance, far above the stands of red spruce, the best in the state, the cell tower lights. This is the signal, night is here, time for sweaters. The temperature can drop forty degrees when the sun goes down. Time for tin-punch constellations, and busy satellites tearing arcs in the sky. Even with the resort and the tower, this is the clearest night you can hope for in the east, as close as you get to that ancient blackness.

Gary says, "Tell Kathryn that. She's moving."

"Moving? Where to?"

"I'm not sure. I was offered a position. At New Mexico State."

Nedermeyer whistles.

"That's what I thought."

"What your folks say?"

"Good question." She visited campus in Las Cruces for a week, taught a class, presented her fisheries research. They loved her—in the swelter, the flatness. Concrete sprawl nibbling at desert, air-conditioning blasting you with its chemical bite. Everyone looking unhealthy and heat-stunned and bleached. She could always come back east in the summer, stay with her mom. She tells herself this as if it solves everything. She doesn't answer Nedermeyer's question.

Gary's half drunk. He says to Nedermeyer, "You folks hungry? We're making dinner."

Michael and Kathryn look at him with curiosity, but he just grins back. So they make a second dinner, and the five of them eat together, filling out the portable table for the first time.

They begin sharing dinner each night, but Shelly keeps on stealing. She and her father stay on for a week, then two. At first they share token supplies—a sliced loaf of store bread, peanut butter—till they run out of food. No one mentions it. Stranger things disappear: a battered water bottle, a bottle opener, a new jug of bleach for sterilizing materials. Nothing expensive: fly rods, the Bushnell rangefinder, and laptops stay put. It feels more like a game than a violation. A magpie of a girl. It doesn't matter. In a week, Kathryn will make the thirty-mile trip to Elkins for supplies.

At this point, her research demands no more than two or three hours a day, so she spends time with Shelly—maybe she's stealing out of boredom. Kathryn takes her swimming in the afternoons, something they both love. The others stay behind to play cutthroat euchre.

Kathryn lends her a towel and they walk to the flat rock by a ruined trestle. The Shavers is a shallow river, and even out in the channel, the water comes only to Kathryn's breastbone. They bring biodegradable soap. They step over a pile of broken crawdads where coons made a meal. The sun is glorious. Mica glitters in the rock.

Kathryn feels a moment's hesitation—taking off her clothes with someone else's child—but in a moment, they're naked. She can't imagine doing this in any other context. Shelly's body is just becoming girlish, winnowing itself out of a child's frame, but naked, she still has a child's lack of self-consciousness. She doesn't know to be ashamed. At seven? Kathryn worries for that, wondering if it has to do with how Shelly was raised. For her part, Shelly gazes full on at Kathryn, a grown woman, unabashed. Esteeming her, those loose breasts, the trim nest of hair. Kathryn doesn't mind, kids are curious, but when they're in the water, she takes care not to touch the girl, not to graze a swimming leg. The rock is pleasant and hot. She loves being naked in the sun. If Gary would leave. Maybe he'll volunteer for Elkins. She tries not to think of sex. She hopes Michael doesn't ask about her father.

They ease in over rounded mossy stones and find the water pleasantly cool, a touch under sixty. Shadows dart to the edge of the pool. Kathryn soaps herself, then hands it over. She wonders if Shelly would have washed otherwise. If Nedermeyer would have cared.

Shelly puts her hand to the current and carves out a white plume of water.

Kathryn closes her eyes for a moment—just a moment—and sinks under. Nedermeyer is telling them about her father. It can't be helped. It nettles just the same. Hell, Nedermeyer is probably related to someone at Green Valley Mine—probably related to *her*. No more than ten thousand people in Tuscarora. When Kathryn was an undergraduate, her father died in the mines. Everyone knows how they were trapped behind a coal rib for eleven hours, before the expired rescue masks failed and methane saturated their lungs. Her mom: *You have to come home, you have to come home.* Kathryn remembers the phone call. At ten in the morning, she was still in bed, groggy from a party, hung over. She still feels guilty, it's the one thing that can make her cry, make her throat burn. Kathryn borrowed a roommate's car and drove feeling drunk, the windows down. She arrived in the clothes she'd slept in, smelling of stale beer. The mine under a siege of news trucks. Shouts, the ragged sound of weeping. Parked cars lining the highway.

In the last moments, her father scrawled a note in huge, amoebic letters: *Don't worry for us. We're not hurting. It's just like falling asleep. I love you all and I will see you in the next world. I will wait on you.* Now her mother lives in that grim pillbox of a house, where her father's hats are lined up neatly on pegs, his work boots nocked in a stand by the door.

A computer says her new office would be 1,887.6 miles from where she sleeps on this mountain. Her mother's house, 37.1. She can leave all this behind. In one swipe of the ax.

Shelly snaps her awake with an awful gutshot howl. *Oh God, she's drowning.* Kathryn claws wet hair from her eyes. A snake shatters the water, a bolt of silver in its mouth. Then Shelly laughs at herself, and Kathryn does too. It races off.

"He ate your fish!"

"That's OK. We'll track him too."

Thirty tagged fish per summer. They made adjustments for mortality. A crass statement: "Adjustments for mortality." Science and its flat, brutal effect.

They climb onto the rock and dry themselves. Kathryn asks for the soap.

"I think I lost it."

It's hidden, of course, under Shelly's folded clothes. Kathryn feels ill, and feels like she would never want a child of her own: the winsome liars. After a long grating pause, she says, "Shelly, if you need anything from me, you just ask, OK? Just ask me. If you want to have lunch or go swimming or get a ride back to town. No games, OK? Don't be shy."

Shelly says OK. Her voice is hollow.

"You don't have to take things."

Kathryn can feel it on her skin. That stinging blush. They are being watched.

"Get dressed. Quick. Someone's coming."

They drag on clothes. They listen. They stare at the laurel hill on the far bank. Nothing.

Kathryn tells herself it was a bear, a bobcat, a doe.

When they get back to the field, Michael has the stove primed and Gary's setting out plates. Nedermeyer isn't around. Was he watching?

He steps out of his tent palming a huge Vidalia onion he forgot he had.

They make omelets for dinner. Nedermeyer laughs at that, but they need to use up the last of their eggs. Red peppers, green peppers, yolk yellow—all the colors of life.

He asks, "How you all paying for this operation?"

Gary—because he wrote the application—brags about the funds they're receiving from the Fish and Wildlife Service, plus a mini-grant from Mead-WestVaCo, a paper conglomerate trying to clean up its image. Trout Unlimited wants to "rebuild" the river, a multimillion-dollar project. A hundred years ago, companies dynamited the boulders and channels to turn the main stem to one big flume. The only deep pools left are a dozen places where railroad trestles cross the river, totally manmade. The winterkill is staggering.

"The pricks," says Nedermeyer. "And we just bend over and let them do it. Beg them to."

"The river can come back," Gary promises him.

Kathryn disagrees. Downstream of here, the resort sloughs so much sediment into the water. It smothers fish eggs in the nest, even in minimal amounts. The only thing that could fix this place is another orogeny, new mountains, glaciation—a cataclysm. But she says nothing.

Nedermeyer croons, "Just give it time, give it time. And this one wants to leave!" He winks at Kathryn. Her eyes go glassy with embarrassment.

Michael flips an omelet expertly. When it's slightly brown, he takes a fork and tips it turtle onto Shelly's plate. She reaches for the catsup and sets out to, as Michael says, ruin a perfectly good omelet. She puts back the catsup. He says, "I was just teasing. Take it."

Nedermeyer asks, "How much river you working?"

"Spruce down to First Fork."

"Superinteresting. I run radar in the navy. Nuclear subs."

"Did you?"

They readjust their feelings toward him. He laughs that musical laugh of his.

"I'd love to see what you do. Shelly says you hurt them but you're awful nice about it."

They decide to tag a fish for the hell of it tomorrow and show off their gear. After dinner, Nedermeyer says, "I wish we could pay you back. Me and Shelly appreciate this."

Gary says, "You'll figure something out."

After inserting the telemeter, Michael slips a dazed nine-inch brook trout into the water. A bronze slash engulfs the poor thing and disappears.

"Jesus! Looked like a fucking water spaniel. About took your hand off, didn't he?"

"Get me the pack," Michael says.

A German brown trout so big the electric shock doesn't even stun it, just sends it jumping and shirking and headshaking, dousing them all. Kathryn leaps on it with both hands. When she lifts the thrashing hook-jawed brown, it disgorges the bedraggled brook trout they just tagged. Michael saves the telemeter, slitting open the sutures. With a digital camera, they take hero shots gripping the fish—a grand female with scarred, scored flanks—and measure her. Over eight pounds, with a girth of fifteen inches. Statistically speaking, a larger fish than this river can support. Like finding a battleship in a parking garage. After wrecking the native trout population, the timber outfits introduced the fast-growing hatchery browns, and they've been here since, in token numbers. Cannibals. They promise to mail Shelly a copy of her picture.

"An outlier," Gary quips.

"That's the fish of a lifetime. A guy'd kill for that. You see a lot like this?"

"No. Not at all. We've caught some nudging twenty-four inches under the other trestles, but nothing like this. Can you imagine her in the fall? She'd carry three pounds of eggs."

Nedermeyer drinks from a battered water bottle, one taken from the researchers' camp. He doesn't bother hiding it. Maybe Shelly told him it was a gift. He hands it to Michael, who takes a drink and says, "Let's track this one too. For the hell of it."

"We don't do invasive species," Kathryn says.

Gary cries, "Listen to the hissing of the sacred geese! Come on. It's a salmonid. I'm just curious. Please. Let us deduce the secrets of the dirty German fish."

"Absolutely not. It would throw off my numbers."

Michael lifts the trout, not quite as gingerly as he would a delicate native trout, to show off its leopard-spotted sides—cracked peppercorns, sunbursts of red, coronas of blue. The underbelly, like rich burnt butter. *Brown*: such a miserly name. The Linnaean, *Salmo trutta*, is so much to be preferred. And the melodic freshwater morpha: *fario*, *lacustris*.

Nedermeyer asks, "You mind if I fish around here?"

The gleaming eyes of an excited fisherman. *Here we go*, Kathryn tells herself. He's seen the fly rods, never used, Gary and Michael brought to the mountain. Like all men and boys in coldwater fisheries, they grew up loving to fish. After a year in the program, they're sick of it. In three summers, Gary has fished all of twice. The electroshocking wand makes fishing silly. It drains the river of mystery, of secrets, when you know what lives there.

Kathryn says coolly, "I didn't know you came here to fish."

"I didn't know this river had big-ass trout in it. Damn."

Gary and Kathryn exchange looks. "Well," she says, "we can't stop you. I mean, we're using these fish to do *research*. I wouldn't want you frying up a mess of our test subjects."

"I'll throw big streamers for big fish. Not your itty-bitty ones. Can I borrow your rod?"

The odds of catching the big female are slim, especially in the clear skinny water of July. Kathryn knows they'll never see the trout again. Let him have his pointless fun.

Michael slips the trout back into the water. Gills rustle, blood-rich. The fins toggle.

"Fuck it," Kathryn says. "Why not? Oh. Sorry Shelly."

"For what?"

Two days later, when Nedermeyer manages to catch that massive trout, they have a late Fourth of July party in celebration. It's enough to feed the five of them, if not fill them. Kathryn sulks a little—not that she's antifishing, she just didn't want to see it killed—until Gary reminds her it's an invasive species, a trash European fish that pops her precious native brook trout like potato chips. A massacre artist! The Ted Bundy of fish! In the scheme of things, a venial sin. She decides to get kind of drunk and let live. They couldn't believe it when Nedermeyer carried the trout into camp. It was long as a lady's stocking. Shelly danced about it, clapping hands.

"What can I say? I got good luck."

After scaling it, Nedermeyer fills the body cavity with sweet onions and a strip of bacon. He wraps the trout in tinfoil and cooks it over the fire on a blackened grillwork. He disdains their portable stove. With raw fire, he bakes potatoes and cinnamon apples and roasts field corn, showing Shelly how to blacken each ear just so. For all his roughness, he's a good doting father. Kathryn fleetingly pictures having a child with him—a thought that dances through her brain like a feather on the wind. The trout's flesh is pink and flaky like a salmon's and falls apart. It has been eating crawdads, and the beta-carotene gives the flesh highlights of reddish richness. With the tines of a fork, Nedermeyer lifts out a delicious cheek and pops it into Shelly's mouth.

It's been a decade, at least, since any of the researchers ate trout.

Afterward, they fire off leftover Roman candles, taking care to stomp out the loose fires that flare in the grass. Balls of light skitter and douse themselves in the river. Gary pulls out his dented pawnshop harmonica and plays the four songs he knows. Wind begins to blow.

A clean linen moon rises over the mountain's worn crest. Swaying a bit, Michael leaves to piss and wash his hands at the river. He's gone a long time. The music manages to be rude, brassy, and sweet. They hear Michael out in the weeds. The world is raucous with tree-frogs.

On nights like this, with music and chill summer air, Kathryn loves West Virginia. There are places on the map called Tennant Run and a Tennant Cemetery in a hollow back of Circleville. Tuscarora County, where people are old-time Republicans and German stock, like her mother, a Propst. The boulder fields, the spaces empty of people—a lonesomeness city dwellers could never comprehend. Sometimes it seems you know animals more intimately than people. Heads of beavers cutting wake in the water, bear scat jeweled with seeds, deer quenching themselves in the river's cool. Her family has lived here for three hundred years. But the place is wretchedly poor and backward and may never be right. She's thirty-one, unmarried and maybe doesn't want to be, with a little tuck in her smile. In a way, Nedermeyer is more correct for her—at least, that's what her home tells her she deserves. Her relatives call her one of those *professional students,* with a touch of teasing, a touch of scorn, a frost-core of jealousy. Even her mother. *You got any men following you around? No? I can't believe that.*

Michael returns, carrying an empty jug he found in the weeds. Clorox. He throws it and hits Nedermeyer square in the chest. In a second, they are standing face to face.

"You dumped bleach in the river. Under the railroad trestle. Come on!"

"Hold on now, I caught that fish, you saw me."

"I didn't see shit! You killed that fish with bleach."

"Shelly saw."

Don't look at her, Kathryn tells herself. This is moving too fast. Everyone knows this county has a grand tradition of fishing with bleach, quarter sticks of dynamite, bottles of carbide.

"There's probably more dead ones. Probably ours."

"Oh my God," Kathryn says.

Nedermeyer begins to blush, and it's hard to tell if it's from anger or embarrassment. "I caught it legal," he says. "I been fishing all my life. It's no trick."

"A gallon of bleach. Do you have any idea how bad this is?"

Shelly has her hands over her ears. She's crying.

"You can't prove that."

Gary smirks and Nedermeyer tells him, "Shut your mouth, fat ass."

Michael lights into him. He calls him a redneck, calls him nine types of motherfucker. "People like you have ruined this place," he says. "Ruined it."

In a book or a movie, this would be the hinge of Shelly's life. The public shaming. Lightheaded now, Kathryn tries to remember a time like this with her dad. All she can recall is a day they went hiking the Elk, and when they returned, a redheaded man with crooked jaw was leaning against their truck. *Thought he was my buddy's. I was fixing to leave a note.* He left walking fast. They found scratches on the paint where he'd tried to pry open the lock with a penknife. Her dad said, *Well you just never know what to expect from people.*

Nedermeyer says, "You finished your speech? You're awful proud of it." He looks to Kathryn and asks her, "Can't you talk some sense into these people?"

She realizes this was supposed to happen, that she would be called on. When nothing comes, he cries, "I knew your dad!"

She doesn't know what to say.

"Come on," Nedermeyer says to his daughter. "I'm not about to expose you to this kind of shit."

Nedermeyer takes her by the hand. They cross the wind-whipped field and leave the researchers to the ruins of their party, to a sudden nip on the wind. Rain. When it comes, the researchers listen to it hissing into the fire.

No one wants to be the first one to slink off to the tents. They stand in silence, till a cracking summer downpour drives them inside, after three weeks of dry, to listen to the wet, deafening roar.

The sun comes up white and indistinct, shining through a gauze of humid sky. The researchers drift from sleep at the same time into a sodden camp. Across the field, the rain-crushed tent shines in the sun. The man and the girl must be miserable.

And they realize the tent has been abandoned. What they see stuns them.

The doors of Kathryn's truck are hanging open.

Their clothes scattered across the field like dead men. The shotgun buried to its chamber in the mud. Their logbooks heavy with rain. A lantern smashed like a melon on a rock. Their laptops flung into the river. Their research wrecked. Nedermeyer and his daughter long gone.

The researchers are numb. Michael says they should take an inventory, so they unload the truck, reckoning up the damage. With a quizzical look, Michael holds up an unopened jug of bleach he finds in the back. The one they thought Shelly stole. He found it under the seat.

By the dead fire, Gary picks up the Clorox from the night before and examines it.

"Oh no."

"What?"

He tips it over and shows them 06/1995 embossed on the bottom. "It was trash," he says in a shy voice. "It wasn't his. It's been here forever."

Back at the state university, the people at computing manage, somehow, to salvage the hard drive from one of the laptops. A minor miracle. Their summer, Kathryn tells everyone, is saved. Then she regrets telling anyone about it at all.

Her paper shows that brook trout, *Salvelinus fontinalis,* in the Shavers Fork of the Cheat River travel an incredible amount—as far as fifty meters a day, and nearly six kilometers up and downriver—though the ones residing in the tributaries keep still, more or less.

Everyone calls it a very fine piece of work. She presents at conferences around North America. The people at New Mexico State send her congratulatory notes.

But that awful morning on the mountain, the project was doomed. Kathryn sprawled on the flat rock, sluggish with guilt and dew-heavy clothes, believing that death is easier than life. In the grand scheme, did it matter? A fish no longer than a salad fork, and botched research, and what a girl thinks of her father. Small things, really. The small geography of their lives.

But it would set her back a year, she thought, another year lost when she felt, rightly or wrongly, that she didn't have many to spare. Kathryn felt sun on her wrists, her neck. She hadn't felt this way since she saw the spidery blue tipple and knew her father was dying underfoot, somewhere, somehow, in that hug of stone. Was she standing on him? Drills, ambulances, mine executives giving their press conference—they meant nothing.

The private road was too muddy to drive on without tearing it up. That was the worst. The researchers had to wait another day to leave the mountain. Again the clouds rolled in.

Rain smacking nylon, the only sound in the world, and not a smudge of light, not even from the tower. Michael didn't come to Kathryn's tent that night. She was disappointed. She hoped he would, so she could turn him back. She had decided to leave this place for good.

DAVID THACKER
Haloed Flotsam

I've watched this ultrasound so often
I close my eyes and picture

a daughter feathered with pixels,
a putto's skeleton. So here is a piece

of art I own, a representation
any impressionist would be proud of

for it moves, though it doesn't yet
move me. But I do return, so she

has achieved what a painting wants:
to be pondered, examined, puzzled over.

If she were a poem, she would be famous
in small, devoted circles. But a child wants

a lizard shellacked with spangles. A child
wants to live on the moon. And what

do I want? What am I? I want to know
when I started seeing every thing

as subject for analysis.
Deep breaths, eyes closed.

Reset the palimpsest,
open—a gray shaking only,

and I'm in the monochromatic
wash of first existence,

hovering above a circle
and two oblong lumps I breathe on.

The circle contracts and swells,
folds in on itself like a mouth,

spits out, for a second, the unmistakable
archipelago of a spine, which disappears.

Here are ribs, waving like coral,
legs and a pelvic girdle,

and just like that I've slipped
through bone, the body

a dim tunnel. I'm turning
through outlines of faint tissue;

I'm where her chin looks down
at the circle around her heart,

and realize my mind's
inside her mind
                    and I shiver.

NANCE VAN WINCKEL
Volunteer

I go around and turn the pages—the newest
news—for the paralytics on the porch.
At least the day isn't hot yet. So says
only a gleam in an old man's eye. A bee
zeroes in for the kill. I roll the ladies
to the shady side. No one wants word
of war. They go for a strangled baby on page three,
continued on page nine, and everything all blue
and purple in between. *I'll show you hot,*
I could say, but I stick a straw between lips.
The stung one needs the first sip. Time to
re-pin my smock's ragged hem and repeat
what I reported yesterday, which no one
believes: *Those ants help the peonies blossom.*

RYAN VINE

Rule 1

do you remember that bum
you ran into

in the bathroom of the Radisson
washing himself with a rag

his clothes in a pile
in the corner

he must have been in his sixties
all smiles and still retarded

by his father's rage
oh this man he said

the things he did
to me and my mother

you wouldn't believe
they made me stronger

and you thought you
knew denial

who are you now
saying you could stop

paying attention
like you had worked

hard enough already
sometimes it's a matter

of feeling yourself
in an elevator

push up through the floors
like a finger through Saran Wrap

or simply a matter of hearing
hillside bells in Little Italy

look
you must remember

the god you chose
opened you like an oven

and placed in you
his favorite dish

to simmer
until you're ready

your head like a buzzer
to take it out

and eat it

EMMA TÖRZS

Come the Revolution

Derek moved into the attic in August, and suddenly there were guns in Lucy's house. Two: a rifle and a shotgun. There was a difference between them, Lucy had learned, though they looked the same to her, both dark-wooded and smoothly tarnished, antique-y, as if they belonged above a mantelpiece instead of propped up in the corner of Derek's messy room. They didn't seem like city guns. City guns were pistols, handguns, were a fierce, sonic crack from the alley outside Lucy's window just as she was falling asleep. Drug dealers, gang members, the motherfucking cops—they had guns. Not anarchist white boys from Eden Prairie.

"That's the point," Derek told her. He was cross-legged on his bed cleaning the rifle, pumping a long metal rod in and out of the barrel. "It's dangerous to have weapons only in the hands of dangerous people. It's dangerous to relegate arms knowledge only to the state."

"Do you ever shoot?" she asked.

He leveled blue eyes at her. "I hope I never have to."

Lucy, too, held this hope. She was a pacifist, a difficult position to maintain among her friends and housemates, who spoke loudly and often of the Revolution—sometimes in joking, abstract terms, and sometimes quite gravely: come the Revolution we'll all eat dirt! Come the Revolution, we'll be lucky to eat at all. There was, in Lucy's community, a recent surge of enthusiasm for such primitive skills as bow-carving and animal-skinning and hide-tanning, and she would sometimes come home and find in her dead-grass backyard a tube of roadkill hides sewn together over a metal pipe to smoke and cure. The hides gave off a pungent, musky fragrance that she found repellant but strangely addictive; at work she would sniff the ends of her hair for it. The modern world seemed to have evolved from a seventies sci-fi novel: the sky was getting hotter by the minute, there was a whirling vortex of trash in the middle of the ocean, like the eye of Sauron, and everywhere she looked she saw eager dough-faced children plugged into machines—computers, video games, iPods—their bodies growing fatter and fatter while their minds shrank in proportion, like apples in an oven. The world seemed destined for horrific collapse, and Lucy was glad to be in the company of people who were preparing for this collapse seriously, even cheerfully.

But she did not like the guns.

The young blind guy in her Wednesday evening Spanish class was a vet—she knew this from the tattoo on his bicep, snakes coiled into the letters USMC—and she found herself watching him, especially his hands. His fingers were always moving, touching, and they were hands that had no doubt gripped a gun; no doubt fired one; no doubt sent a bullet roaring into someone's life, to take it. Not a gun like Derek's rust-barreled antiques, but the kind of gun Lucy pictured when she imagined being held at the point of one.

He—the blind guy, James—was new to the class, just three Wednesdays under his belt, and he had a frequent, grateful laugh. Yet every time he spoke, Lucy thought, *You've killed people.* She'd known plenty of boys who'd gone *to* war, mostly kids in her high school, but she knew few people who'd *been.* She assumed he'd lost his sight in combat, and she wondered if he was religious, if he'd taken the injury as a sign of punishment from God: what could be more biblical than being struck blind for murder? But then, she wasn't too familiar with the Bible.

On James' fourth Wednesday, she asked the group, in her unpolished Spanish, "What's the worst thing you've ever done?"

James said, "Kissed my best friend Adam's girlfriend."

This was not the answer Lucy was looking for. But what person, while sitting at a beat-up wooden high school desk in a dingy back room of the Center for Peace and Learning would say to a group of strangers, "The worst thing I've ever done is *kill a man.*" Drumroll.

She was no good at coaxing people to speak, anyway. During these classes she would pose a question and the group would stare as if she'd asked them to turn handsprings. Admittedly she was not the best choice to lead these language circles. But of the few people who'd applied, she was the only who appeared "authentic," though in truth she'd never lived outside the Minneapolis city limits. Appearances, as always, were everything. Except if you were blind.

"Where did you learn Spanish?" James asked her after class. He was still seated at his undersized desk, backpack on his lap and those big hands roving over the front pocket until they found the zipper and pulled.

"My father's from Ecuador," she said, watching him unfold his white cane. "But he left when I was ten and I only spoke English after that."

"I was in the hospital a couple years ago," he said, and gestured to his face, to the scars unraveling like thread from the corners of his eyes. "My mother brought in these tapes she found at a garage sale. Spanish instruction tapes. The lady on the tape, she didn't talk anything like you. She pronounced all her double-Ls like Sh. Like she was saying *Asia* instead of *ella*. I thought it was normal but I guess it's not."

"They speak like that in some places. Argentina, I think."

"It sounds like she's trying to get something out of her teeth." He sent a dimpled grin in her direction. "I like the way you talk. It's a lot rockier."

She felt her face grow warm. "That's a good thing?"

He got to his feet, cane in one hand, backpack slung across the other shoulder. The rest of the class was gone and they were alone in the dingy room.

"If you like rocks," he said.

That night, Lucy went down the hall to Elaine's room and stretched out next to her bed, Elaine already beneath the covers. The floor was covered in hides, roadkill from all over Minnesota, and they gave the bedroom a rich medieval air. The crowning glory was a coyote whose clever face was still intact, and Lucy lay down on him, buried her nose in the soft dead fur of his head. He had that same earthy, genital smell that all the hides gave off, but his was deeper, more intricate. Lucy had cried when Elaine brought the body home, curled up in the trunk of the car. All four of his legs had been broken, and when Elaine stripped back his skin, his insides were hamburger.

"At least he's being put to use," Elaine had said. "Instead of rotting by the side of the road."

Lucy wasn't sure her own definition of *use* included being an ornamental rug, but she loved the hide, and she tried to love the coyote who had once inhabited it, as if her love could somehow soothe whatever cosmic wound his death had left in the skin of the world.

"Elaine," she said. "Have you ever killed anything? Aside from bugs."

Elaine hung her chin over the edge of the bed. "No."

"Would you describe my voice as *rocky?*"

"What? No?"

"Do you know any blind people?"

"No. Ask me something I can say yes to."

Lucy reached up and tugged a lock of Elaine's tangled hair. It was a coppery auburn that bleached orange in the sun, and was cut short on one side so she seemed a different person depending on the angle. "There's a blind guy in one of my Spanish classes," Lucy said. "He was in the war."

"Which war?"

"This one. He's a nice guy. I mean, he's just a normal person, doesn't seem political one way or the other."

"I can't imagine killing people in the name of something I don't care about."

"I can't imagine killing anyone, period," Lucy said. She stared up at the glow-in-the-dark stars Elaine had spread in asterisms across her ceiling. Even with the lamp on they held a suffused, plastic kind of warmth, as if they were collecting light for later. Truth was, she *had* imagined killing people. No one specific, just a long list of ifs: If someone tried to rape her. If someone tried to hurt her mother, or her friends. If someone were going to kill a lot of people unless you killed him first. But when she thought of killing, it was never with a gun. Always fists—a nose crunching upward into the brain, a head slammed onto concrete. Something human.

"Sort of speaking of," Elaine said after a moment. "Derek's going up North next weekend. For that marksmanship training clinic. Did you see the flier on the fridge? Women shoot for free. I think I'm going to go—you should come. It'd be a good skill to get down."

Lucy looked up at her. "What? When would you ever need to shoot a gun?"

"Well," Elaine said, "when do you ever *need* to hear a song? But I never asked why you took guitar lessons last year."

"If you learn to shoot," Lucy said, "would you go hunting?"

"If I needed to. Not otherwise."

If. If food supplies were scarce or guarded. If the city blew up. If the world went down.

"Great," Lucy said. "You can hunt our dinner, and I'll…" She couldn't think of something to offer.

"You'll play 'Blackbird' every night. You'll keep us human."

Lucy put a finger through the dried-up hole of the coyote's eye. "Why would I want to do that?" she said.

The next Wednesday, James stayed behind after class again.

"My buddy works at the coffee shop two blocks down," he said. "Want to come get a free fancy drink?"

It was 6:30, fading light, warm, and the streets were busy. Briefcased men and pencil-skirted women clustered at the bus stops, eyes fixed to their watches or cellphones to avoid the gazes of the shabbier people fringed around them like the edges of burned paper. Everyone seemed choppy and insubstantial, digital figures in a 2D cityscape, and in their midst Lucy felt hollowly alive. The café was one she'd walked past many times but never entered, and James led her to a pair of couches in the back, orange corduroy with overstuffed cushions. He navigated the space with hesitant, practiced taps of his cane, like someone going through the steps of a dance he'd only just begun to learn, and his competence was exhausting—Lucy was tightrope-tense trying not to be afraid for him.

They sat down kitty-corner, a couch each.

"Where are you?" James asked.

"Here."

He turned his head toward her. His eyes were hazel and a little cloudy, like resin. "You wanna hear something sad?" he said. "Spanish class is the highlight of my week."

She huffed a laugh. "That *is* sad."

"Goes to show you how boring my summer's been. Never thought I'd be so psyched for school to start up again." He took a sip of his drink, an elaborate mocha. It was hard to reconcile the dual images she held of him: imaginary James had a machine gun hoisted to his shoulder, while the one before her had whipped cream on his chin.

"So," James said. "What's the highlight of your week?" He patted the table in front of him and set down his mug.

"Depends on the week, I guess," she said. "This one's more exciting than usual. Tomorrow my friend's having a birthday party for her kid— he's turning two. I'm told there will be beer and a bouncy castle."

"Solid."

"And this weekend I'm going camping."

He straightened. "Yeah? Where?"

"Up North, on Superior. My friends are doing this marksmanship clinic, though I'm just going along for the camping, not to shoot. I'm not big into guns."

"Your friends are?"

"My friends…" She blew on the hot dark surface of her coffee. "My friends want to know they can take care of themselves, if it comes to that."

"Like, the Tea Party?"

"No! God, no. They're punk radical, not Tea Party radical."

James sat forward, elbows on his splayed knees. "Radical is radical," he said. "Sounds fun. I haven't been camping in years. Not since before I fucked up my eyes."

Oh, how she wanted to ask. Wanted to *know,* in gory, intimate detail.

"We have space in the car," she said, pulse quickening. "You could come, if you wanted."

"Nah," James said. A hectic flush rose from under the neck of his T-shirt and crept up his throat.

"Really," she said. "We've got an extra sleeping bag."

"But," he said. "I can't—I can't help with the driving, or anything."

"It's only three hours away."

He shook his head.

"Come on," she said. "It'll be super low-key. Just the three of us, and you."

"You really wouldn't mind me tagging along?" he said, finally.

"Not in the least."

He passed a finger across the scuffed tabletop to re-find his drink, and said, "All right." The color faded back down under his shirt. "Why not."

"Done deal," she said, and clapped once.

"I don't know what's weirder," Elaine said. "That you invited him or that he said yes."

"He was in the Marines?" Derek said. "Does he know what we're about?"

"Sure," Lucy said. "He's a very open guy."

They were sitting up in Derek's attic with the guns. Two floors down, their landlord, Ken, was knocking on the door; Lucy could see the top of his baseball cap from the triangular attic window. There'd been a spate of foreclosures in Minneapolis, and they didn't want bad news—three of their friends had been evicted in the past four months. Lately, Ken seemed haggard and demanding, enforcing things he'd never cared about before: watering the sparse grass, repainting the front steps, keeping the bikes off the porch. Elaine said maybe he wanted to kick them out and rent the house at a higher price so he could make the mortgage.

"I should go down there with this," Derek said, and patted his rifle.

"Not funny," said Lucy.

"I heard about this punk house in New Orleans during Katrina," Derek said. "It was a mostly black neighborhood, and the cops wouldn't lift a finger to help when shit got crazy. The punks were the only house on the block with guns, and they defended the whole neighborhood."

"I don't think we need to defend ourselves against Ken," Elaine said. "He's the wimpiest guy on earth."

"Not Ken," Derek said. "But I'm just saying. It's good to be ready to protect what's ours. Our home, our friends, our neighborhood."

"You sound like a commercial for the army," Lucy said. "*Protect what's ours.* Hear me roar."

"Except the army wants to protect the government. We want to protect ourselves *from* the government, who want to protect themselves from us."

"It's just a big circle of protection, then. A giant, messy violence-condom."

Derek laughed and patted her on the knee, and Lucy smacked his hand away. "Got to protect what's mine," she said.

James lived with his mother in St. Paul, and it was she who answered the door early Saturday morning. She was blond and hen-shaped, and instead of shaking hands she dug her fingers into Lucy's shoulder. "You'll be back tomorrow?" she said to her son. "It's just one night?"

"I'm not going over this with you again," James said. Under his mother's low ceiling he looked both oversized and diminished, like a giant's child. At the doorway he took Lucy's arm, his grip loose in the crook of her elbow, and she felt anxious at the reliance implicit in his touch. She hadn't signed on to babysit.

"I've always been a worrier," his mother said. "Always."

"Nice to have met you," Lucy said.

She'd never led a blind person before and was clumsy as they made their way down the gravel walkway to the idling car. Elaine watched their progress through the open window of the passenger seat, her face all gleeful curiosity.

"Here we are," Lucy said. "The handle is right at your hip."

James fumbled for a moment, and then his fingers found the metal lever and he tugged it open, felt out a space for his duffle bag before lowering himself in.

"Hey," Elaine said. "I'm Elaine."

"I'm Derek," said Derek, and added, "I'm driving."

"James," said James. He was sitting up very straight, shoulders tense. "Thanks for letting me come along. Gonna learn how to shoot some guns, huh? Yeehaw."

"You know it," Derek said, and hesitated, as if about to say something else, then threw the car into gear. Elaine turned around, appraised James openly. Raised her eyebrows at Lucy, who shook her head, feeling color in her cheeks.

"So, James," Elaine said. "You go to the U?"

"I'm going to need to know what you're wearing," James said. "Standard procedure."

"What?" Elaine said. "Uh—black jeans?"

"Just playing," said James. "Yeah, I go to the U."

The ride wasn't as uncomfortable as Lucy had feared, though Derek and Elaine seemed disproportionately impressed each time James made a joke, and they made good time from the city. It was a little after noon by the time they got the tent up and the firewood collected; the clinic began at one. Elaine wandered off down the dirt road, "exploring," while Derek spread a dirty blanket on the pine needles and hunkered down to strip and clean his rifle; Lucy smelled the tang of metal and gun oil in the hot air. As far as she could tell, the cleaning was a useless exercise, since the gun was never fired. She picked up a box of ammo and shook a few heavy bullets out into her palm, rolling them back and forth. "Here," she said to James, cross-legged beside her, and he held out his hand.

"Twenty-two?" he said.

"Yep." Derek looked up. "It's an old Remington—from the '30s, I think. Belonged to my grandpa."

James pinched a bullet between two fingers. "Can I take a look when you're done?"

If Derek felt the same unease that Lucy did at the turn-of-phrase, he didn't show it. "Sure," he said, and nudged the butt into James' knee. James hefted it, then ran a hand down the barrel, explored the curve of the trigger and the spring of the safety. His touch was certain. Goose-bumps flickered up Lucy's bare arms.

"Bet she's pretty," James said.

"Plain, but elegant," Derek said.

"My grandmother used to shoot rabbits with a rifle like this." James skimmed a hand over the blanket in front of him and picked up one of the bullets, and with quick, steady movements he dropped it into the breech and swung the butt up to rest on his shoulder, one blind eye to the scope.

Derek's hand came up. "Careful, man."

"It's OK," James said, his finger nestled on the trigger. "The safety's on."

The barrel was pointed right between Derek and Lucy, where Elaine was walking toward them through the trees, oblivious. Lucy held herself still, though her heart was pounding.

"We should probably get going," Derek said. "It's almost one."

James lowered the rifle back down on the blanket. Derek zipped it quickly into its leather case, and Elaine picked up the shotgun from where it lay among the leaves.

"Ready when you are," Elaine said, and squeezed Lucy's shoulder. "You guard the camp while we're gone."

"If by *guard* you mean *drink beer*, then I've got you covered."

Lucy watched them set off through the trees, their gun cases hanging down their backs. They looked adorable and stupid.

A prissy, robotic female voice announced, "It is twelve forty-two p.m." Lucy turned to see James close his cellphone.

"Do you want to go down by the water?" she asked.

"Sure," he said, pushing himself up. "Lead on."

She took him by the arm, his muscle jumping beneath her fingers. "Actually," he said, "it's easier for me if I hold onto you."

"Oh," she said. "Sorry. I don't really know how to do this."

"Just tell me if I'm about to step off a cliff."

At the water he let her arm go and crouched down, fingers creeping along the gravelly sand until they hit the tide. "Damn," he said. "It's freezing."

Lucy knelt beside him. From the thin sandy beach the water stretched out like a greedy mirror, collecting the blue of the sky and the herds of clean, white clouds. She'd been to the ocean, once in California and twice in North Carolina, but she preferred the great lakes—they smelled cleaner, less full of salty dead.

She put a hand in, felt the cold, and heard the crack of a gunshot from across the lake, echoing off the water. James jumped up so quickly she thought for a second he'd been hit.

"What was that?" he said.

"Probably the marksman clinic," Lucy said. "They're a little early, but—"

Another sharp report rang across the water. James flinched. "Are they going to be doing that all afternoon?"

Another shot, then another, then a volley. James raised his hands toward his ears but didn't cover them. "Shit," he said. "That's really fucking loud."

Lucy touched his back. "Maybe, if we move away from the water."

"Yeah," he said, "yeah," and he reached out for her. She caught his wet fingers, placed them on her arm, and they scrambled up the embankment. Away from the lake the shots came just as loud. At the edge of the orange blanket, James dropped her arm and spun on his heel in a half circle, hands up by his ears again but still not touching. Shots kept coming.

"James," Lucy said, "they're far away. They're not going to hit us."

His eyes were squeezed shut. "Sorry," he said, "I'm sorry, I just don't like it. Fuck, I really don't like it."

"If you covered your ears...?"

"I'm blind," he said, "I don't want to be deaf too. *Fuck*."

"Why don't we get in the car," Lucy said. "We can turn on some music really loud, and drive somewhere for a while. Do you want to do that?"

He shook his head. "Yeah, OK. Yeah."

In the passenger seat he sucked in a few deep breaths; his knuckles were white on his knees. Lucy turned on the radio and a jangly country song blared from the speakers. He lurched forward and smacked at the console with an open palm.

"Turn it off," he said.

The car pitched down the dirt road, shots fading behind them. By the time they hit the smooth pavement of the county highway, the only noise was the hum of the car and James' jagged, controlled breathing. For a while they drove without speaking, James still rigid beside her, but eventually his shoulders came down from around his ears and he leaned back against the headrest.

"I'm going to pull over up here," Lucy said. "There's like a little picnic area. Is that OK? Or do you want to keep driving."

"Yeah," James said, and blew out a tired breath. "Pull over."

She jolted off the pavement back onto dirt, eased the car into the grassy space beside the picnic table. It was supposedly a scenic over-look, but the only view was of dense trees and a distant edge of water, and the only sound was the faint ticking of the engine.

"Listen," James said. "I'm really sorry about that."

"You don't have to apologize," she said.

"I'm not usually so jumpy." He angled his body toward her. "Thanks for being cool."

"It comes naturally."

"Freaking out doesn't," he said. "That, you have to learn." He squinted at her, as if it would help him see. "So what scares *you*, tough girl? Or are you just level all the time?"

She paused, then said, "People." She watched the tap-tap-tap of his fingers on his thigh. "People in general. We do terrible things."

He pulled a sharp breath in through his nose. "In class you said the worst thing you've done is wreck your mother's car." His fingers moved faster. "Is that true?"

"Probably not. It's just the first thing I thought of."

"Me too," James said. "Mine was the first thing I thought of. But I've done worse." He rolled his shoulders, as if readying himself in a ring. "It's pretty fucked up that the first thing that came to mind was kissing Adam's girlfriend when I was sixteen. Bet that's not what you wanted to hear, is it? When you asked in class?"

She was silent. He was right. She had wanted to hear him—what? Confess? Confirm? But she felt terrible guilt now, for having wanted.

"Really, though," James said. "What scares you more than anything? What would make you run?"

His hands were clenched and he was leaning toward her, his jaw working. Lucy felt the smallness of the space, the car pressing down around them like a closing fist, but through the windshield she could see a hint of pristine lake, and beyond the water was the Minnesota sky; not a vast blue ceiling, as she'd imagined as a child, but something open—something that looked back at her. The constant eye of the unblinkable world.

"Sometimes I feel so safe," she said.

Visit #1

Your grandfather and I walk alike,
each of us counting the brittle spaces
in getting older. At the desk I explain
I want to see my son, and I see you
are now digits on a sheet. Black
men in black—the brothers—make sure
you obey the rules. It is like the times
I had to come to school to get you
for being bad. Being bad is the name
of this place and this place is the city
itself. Stars in the night are for escaping.
If you can touch one, you can crawl
out of this city, out of falling down.

In the doorway you come batting
back tears. It is the Detention Center,
not school, not the principal, but men
with violence as hope. My father
and I have come to see you, and we
so much want you to outlive us.
To bury you would pull us down
into the spiked pit of grief that kills.

So we laugh to make you laugh,
but you only cry because you know
we tried to teach you the good.
I pray for you. It is my only secret.
Black men in black count
the smiles we give you.

ERIC WEINSTEIN

One Good King

Then the Great Dane became
an arrow of smoke in a wind

pipe of smoke, so I had to burn
the body. He'd always considered

himself king of infinite dominions:
king of the bone, king of the living

room, king of the elevator, king
of the field. The ashes I scattered

in a park close to home, in case
there are such things as ghosts

and his goes in search of the
familiar. So his ghost won't dig

for his own bones each evening.
I don't believe in anyone

but him. I don't believe in anything
but this: that after this life

there is a valley or a hall, a waiting
room or train platform or field

to be reigned over, a ball or stick
to cast out and retrieve, every hour wide

as it is long—the game going on and on,
the day broad and spotless as the heart of a dog.

STEPHEN NEAL WEISS
Arriving at the End

The Tartars say: After the wedding, we don't need the music.

And in Yiddish it is said: It's the last one whom the dogs attack.

The Italians say: The last to arrive must shut the door.

The English say: The last suitor wins the maid.

They also say: No one has ever seen tomorrow.

Spaniards say: Tomorrow is often the busiest day of the week.

The Germans say: A little late is much too late.

And in Latin it is said: Those who come late get the bones.

The Danish say: It's too late to come with water when the house has
burned down.

They also say: It's too late to cover the well when the child has
drowned.

The French say: It's too late to lock the stable door when the horses
are gone.

Americans say: It's too late to learn to box when you're already in the
ring.

They also say: The cage is ready but the bird has flown.

Ovid said: Too late do I take up the shield after the wound.

XUAN JULIANA WANG
Days of Being Mild

It takes real skill to speed down the packed streets of Zhongguancun, but the singer with the mohawk is handling it like a pro. His asymmetrical spikes are poking the roof of his dad's sedan, so he's compensating by tilting his head slightly to the left.

We are meeting with a new band to talk about possibly shooting their music video. Sara is here to deal with the script details and she is leaning all the way forward to talk concept with the two guys up front. Sara's long blond hair is wavy and tumbling down her skinny back and Benji's got his fingers in her curls. His other hand is pinching a cigarette, arm out the window.

I'm staring at the women rhythmically patting their babies while selling counterfeit receipts, and I can hear taxi drivers asking about each other's families as their cars slide back and forth. Teenage part-timers are throwing advertisements in the air like confetti and somehow we're managing not to kill anyone.

The band's name is Brass Donkey and they're blasting their music from the sedan's tiny speakers. They sound a lot like Jump In On Box, the all-girl orbit-pop band that just got signed to Modern Sky Records. I'm digging the sound but nobody asks for my opinion.

We finally make our way to the singer Dao's apartment and more band members show up. He sits us down on the couch, and even though it's only noon, he offers us Jack Daniels and Lucky Strikes. There are piles of discs everywhere and stacks of DVD players that the bootleg DVDs keep breaking.

"So this video, we want it to really stand out. We're really into the Talking Heads right now, you know them? Talking Heads?"

The drummer turns on the TV and David Byrne appears, jerking his face back and forth to the beat of the music. All the band members are talking to us at once.

"We're no wave Funstrumental, but we sound Brit Pop."

"For this video we want something perversely sexual, like really obscene and perverse."

They look expectantly at Benji and Sara.

"Yeah, like really fucking sick, you know?"

"The more perverted the better!"

"Then we want this video to be blasting in the background during our big winter performance at Star Live, on the big monitors."

I smoke their cigarettes. "Aren't you afraid of the police coming in and shutting it down?"

"That would be spec-fuckin-tacular! It would be great to be shut down, even better if you could get us banned. Actually, let's make that a goal," said the singer, sinking back into his chair, turning up the music.

I watch Sara look down at her notes and then look up at me. I shrug whatever, and Benji stands up to leave and shakes everybody's hand. Then we're out of there. I can't wait to tell JJ and Ah Ming; they'd definitely get a kick out of this story.

As for the video, we'll do it if we feel like it, see how it goes.

We are what the people called *Bei Piao*—a term coined to describe the twenty-somethings who drift aimlessly to the northern capital, a phenomenal tumble of new faces to Beijing. We are the generation who awoke to consciousness listening to rock and roll, and who fed ourselves milk, McDonalds, and box sets of *Friends*. We are not our parents, with their loveless marriages and party-assigned jobs, and we are out to prove it.

We come with uncertain dreams, but our goal is to burn white hot, to prove that the Chinese, too, can be decadent and reckless. We are not good at math or saving money, but we are very good at being young. We are modern-day May Fourth–era superstars, only now we have Macbooks. We've read Kerouac in translation. We are marginally employed and falling behind on our filial piety payments, but we are cool. Who was going to tell us otherwise?

Five of us live in part of a reconverted pencil factory outside the fourth ring, smack in the middle of the 798 art district. We call our place The Fishtank, and it covers four hundred square meters of brick and semiexposed wall insulation. Before it became our home, it used to function as the women's showers for the factory workers.

As a result, it is cheap and it is damp. The real Beijing, with its post-Olympic skyscrapers, stadiums, and miles of shopping malls, rests comfortably in the distance, where we can glance fondly at the glow of lights while eating lamb sticks.

The roommates include JJ, the tall, dark-skinned half-Nigerian from Guangzhou, who is loud-mouthed and full of swagger. He keeps his head shaved, favors monochromatic denim ensembles, and is either drinking or playing with his own band Frisky Me Tender. The resident cinematographer is Benji, who is so handsome waitresses burst into fits of giggles when taking his orders. He is working on a series of migrant workers whom he dresses in designer labels. Benji, whose Chinese name we've forgotten, was renamed by his white girlfriend, Sara, a former research scholar who has since found it impossible to leave. Sara, with her green eyes and blond hair, spoke with an authentic marbled Northeastern Chinese accent, and somewhere along the line, she became one of us as well. There is Ah Ming from Xiamen, the photographer who shoots product photos of new consumer electronics, as well as an ever-rotating roster of models from Russia and Hong Kong. Some of them keep us company when they are sufficiently drunk. Then there's me and I'm short like Ah Ming, but based on appearances, sometimes I can't help but feel as though someone accidentally photographed me into this picture.

I'm a so-called producer, and what that really means is just that I have more money than the rest of them. Actually my dad does. My family's from Chong Qing, where my dad made a fortune on real estate and has more money than he can spend. Since I dropped out of Beijing Film Academy over a year ago, I've been hiding from my dad and am now living off the money I got from selling the BMW he gave me. I said I'd try to make it as a filmmaker, but I'm low on talent. Lately, I've been watching a lot of porn.

Our apartment is just around the corner from our new favorite bar See If, and that's where Benji, Sara, and I go after our meeting. See If is three stories of homemade wood furniture and Plexiglas floors. The drinks are named "if only," "if apart," "if together," "if no if," and so on. The alcohol is supposed to complement your mood, but it basically all tastes the same. JJ and Ah Ming and a bunch of part-time male models are all there with guitars strapped on. JJ is walking around suggestively strumming everyone's guitars.

Benji says to the group, "Hey, you have to hear the story about our meeting with the Brass Donkey guys. I think they want to get publicly flogged."

I get passed a pipe and I smoke something that makes me feel vaguely like I'm in trouble. I concentrate on looking at my friends and feel swell again.

JJ cuts in, "Dude, today a cab driver point-blank asked me how big my dick was." We listen to that story instead. Being a half-black Chinese guy, JJ is used to attention.

With the 2008 Olympics finally behind us, Beijing is getting its loud, open-mouthed, wise-cracking character back. The cops stopped checking identity papers on the street and all of us Bei Piao let out a collective sigh of relief. We were getting back to life as usual.

But then this thing happened. Last week I received an e-mail from my father. He was going to give me, his only son, the opportunity to make my own fortune. He purchased a dozen oilrigs in Louisiana and has hired an agency to get the L-1 investment visa ready for me to move there and manage it. It has been decreed that my piece of shit ass is going to move to the U.S. and make use of itself. In his mind, what was I doing drifting around in Beijing with hippies when there's an oil field in Louisiana with my name on it?

We test shoot the video on our roof, and even though it's a Wednesday, I make a few calls to modeling agencies and within the hour, half a dozen models are strutting across our tiles, wearing nipples and fishnets. Sara's the one posing them in obscene variations, asking them to take their clothes off. She can get away with almost anything because she's a white girl who speaks Chinese and everybody likes her. Benji's doing the actual filming while Ah Ming takes stills. Sometimes I load some film, but mostly I just drink beer and enjoy the atmosphere.

Just as the sun is whimpering its way down the side of the sky, the last girl shows up. She is a model from Hong Kong who renamed herself Zi Guang, The Light. She has a good face but like most girls who assume they deserve nice things, she is extremely unfriendly. Then, just as everyone is packing up to go, she emerges from the apartment naked and wrapped in Ah Ming's blue bed sheet. Her waist-length black hair licks at her face, her arms gather the bouquet of fabric against her small breasts, and the sheet clings to the silhouette of her long legs. Among our coffee cups and cigarettes, the rest of us hardly notice her, smile at her but not much more.

Not Ah Ming. He picks up his medium-format lens, ties his hair into a ponytail, and follows her onto the tile roof like a puppy.

He takes her hand, and helps ease her bare feet onto the chimney. With the sheet dripping down from her, she looks ten feet tall and glorious. She lowers the sheet and ties it around her waist, covers herself with her hair and looks away, purring like a cat, in a halfhearted bargain for attention.

So there's Ah Ming, between whose lips escapes a "My God," and he fumbles with filters and straps to get the perfect photo of her. The loose tiles creak underneath his feet.

"You're beautiful, too beautiful," he says. "You should father my children or marry me, whatever comes first."

Sara whispers to me, "I think this is going to be trouble." And I know just as well as everyone else that Ah Ming's falling for this girl, and it isn't going to be pretty.

If we could grant Ah Ming one wish, he'd probably say he'd wish to marry a tall girl. A very tall, very hot, girl. He claims that he wants to give his children a fighting chance. Can we really blame him though? Even if he only claimed to be of average male size, he's probably only 5 foot 3—in the morning, after he's taken a big breath and held it. Most of the time, the poor guy has to buy shoes in the children's department.

But all that is bullshit; it's just for show. Ah Ming, perpetually heartbroken Ah Ming, is the only one of us who can still memorize Tang Dynasty poetry, is always the first to notice if sorrow crosses any of our faces. I guess deep down we could all see that his wants were so simple—to be loved, respected, and not tossed away, for his meager holdings on this earth. It was all the wrong in him that made him so special, and we were all protective of him, and ready to hurt for him as we would hurt for no one else.

After the shoot is over, we go across town to D-22 to hear JJ's band perform. D-22 is the first underground punk rock club literally screamed into existence by foreign exchange students in the university district. JJ is opening for Car Sick Cars, whose hit song is a five-minute repetitive screaming of the words "Zhong Nan Hai," which is both the Beijing capitol building and the most popular brand of cigarettes among locals. Foreigners love it, and the audience throws cigarettes onto the stage like projectile missiles.

When JJ and his band hit the stage, it's obvious that he's wasted. He tips the mike stand over as he gyrates in his Adidas tracksuit. He is singing in English, "I trim girls all night long, white and black, I know how to trim those." These lyrics are new, they're probably bits of conversation he said earlier that day, grammatically Chinese and English, clauses that don't finish, lyrics that don't make sense. It's Cantonese slang for "hit on girls," coarsely translated to English, being yelled through a broken mike. We all know he kind of sucks, but so does everybody else and everyone's liking it. The Chinese groupies who took day-long buses into the city just to see the show are thrashing their heads back and forth as if they're saying, "No No No" when they're really saying "Yes Yes Yes." JJ finishes the set by jumping off the stage and feeling up a drunk Norwegian girl who doesn't seem to mind.

Like everyone else I know, JJ drinks a ton. Unlike everyone else, he doesn't seem to want to make it big. He says he just doesn't see the use of being a hardworking citizen. I certainly can't argue with that. I know most ordinary people will work their whole lives at some stable job and they'll never be able to afford so much as a one-bedroom in Beijing proper.

When the next band starts plugging in their instruments, Sara goes to mingle with the Canadian promoter, while JJ joins Benji and me by the bar.

"I am not writing for record labels. I just want to write music for the humiliated loser, the guy that gets hassled by the police, the night owl with no money, who loves to get fucked up," JJ says. I don't know if he knows that his description doesn't include someone like me, but we toast to that anyway.

Next we all go clubbing in Sanlitun at a place called Fiona. A once-famous French architect purportedly designed it in one hour. Every piece of furniture is a unique creation, and as a result, it looks like a Liberace-themed junkyard. Bamboo, an old acquaintance who runs a foreign modeling agency, is throwing a birthday party for herself.

"Can you believe I'm turning 29 again?" she says as a greeting while she ushers us into her private room. She kisses everyone on the mouth and presses little pills into our hands.

"Oh, to be young and beautiful, I can't think of anything more fabulous," she says, in her signature mixture of Chinese and English, as she drapes her arms around a new model boyfriend. His name is Kenny or Benny, and he looks like a skinny Hugh Jackman. He is obviously a homosexual, but that's just not something Bamboo has to accept.

The DJ spins funky house tracks, and the springboard dance floor floods with sweaty people who pant and paw at each other. Old businessmen drool at foreign girlfriends who lift up their skirts in elevated cages. Bamboo buys the drinks and toasts herself into oblivion, grooving around the dance floor, yelling at the foreigners to "Go nuts to apes and shit!"

I can't find Ah Ming or Benji, so instead I try striking up a conversation with skinny Hugh Jackman. He asks me to teach him Chinese, so I start by pointing to the items on the table.

"This is a bowl," I say.

"Bowa! Ah Bowl!" he says with a shit-eating grin on his face.

"Shot glass." I push it across the table toward him.

"Shout place," he slurs, laughing. "Oh yeaah, shout place!"

It's a good thing he's handsome, I think. I want to leave but I'm too high to wander around looking for my friends. I stick by the bar for a little bit and talk to the attractive waitresses who swear they've met me before, in another city, in another life, and I am sad that they have nothing to say to me but lies.

Beijing is a city that is alive and growing. At any given moment, people are feasting on the streets, studying for exams, or singing ballads in KTVs. Somewhere a woman with a modest salary is buying thousand-yuan pants from Chloé to prove her worth. Even though I couldn't cut it at Beijing Film Academy, I knew the city itself was for me. The dinosaur bones found underneath shopping malls, the peony gardens, the enclaves of art, these things were all exhilarating for me. I walk through new commercial complexes constructed at Guomao, which look at once like big awkward gangsters gawking at each other, as if hesitant to offer each other cigarettes, and I think, *I belong here.*

Tonight, I somehow end up crawling out of a cab to throw up by the side of the freeway. Traffic swirls around me, even though the morning light's not fully up. Then out of the blue, Sara and Benji appear, apparently because they happened to see my big shaved head projectile vomiting as their cab was passing. They pat me on the back and, on the side of the road, we eat hot pot from an old Xin Jiang lady. I am so happy to be with them. It's at this moment I realize that what's going on is already slipping away, and while the cool air blows against my damp face on the taxi home, I can't help but miss it already.

One night, my last real girlfriend, Li Qiang, calls me.

"I'm moving to Shanghai next month, and I'm wondering if you could lend me some money to get settled. You know I'm good for it," she says. She knows more about me than anyone and there's not even a hiccup of hesitation in her voice.

That's just how Li Qiang did things. The girl couldn't just sit on a chair, she had to lie in it, with her head cocked to the side and a cigarette dangling dangerously. She is a sound mixer I met at the academy, and always dressed as if she had a Harley parked out back. Her playground was Mao's Live House, where she rejoiced in the last blaze of China's metal head scene.

There was never going to be a future for us; my father would have never accepted a poor musician into the family. Yet it was she who dumped me, simply saying, "I wish I could give you more. You should have more."

I meet her for coffee and hand her an envelope of money and she accepts it as though it's a book or a CD. She has cut her hair like a boy, but she is still fiercely beautiful and radiant as ever.

"We're doing well, you know," I say. "Benji's trying to get British art dealers to buy his photographs and Sara's in talks with a Dutch museum to exhibit her media installation. And Ah Ming just got published in a Finnish fashion magazine."

She goes, "That's impressive, but what are *you* doing?"

My throat is dry, and I'm not sure what to say, so I go, "I'm in between projects."

"Of course," she says, reaching over and messing up my hair.

Ah Ming's relationship with Zi Ying isn't normal either. Two days after they met, she moved into his room and began spending all her time on his bed. It is so weird in there even the pets stay away. For one, she would walk around topless, one minute laughing, the next waking us up with bawls.

"That girl should be taking antidepressants," Sara said.

In the mornings, Zi Ying tells Ah Ming she loves him, and he believes it. In the afternoons, she says he is disgusting to her and he believes that too. "You can't just pick and choose," he tells us. "When you're trying to get someone to love you, you have to take everything." When she sleeps with him, he marvels at all the soft places on her body he can kiss. It amazes him how easily he bruises when she kicks him away.

Ah Ming's website quickly becomes a shrine to Zi Ying's face. She is so crazy and beautiful it's as if she stole his eyes and hung them above her at all times. Gone are all the projects he'd been working on, and we hardly see him without her. It is only Zi Ying, her in the bathtub with goldfish, her on his bed with broken liquor bottles, lovingly captured and rendered over and over again.

We send each other his links over QQ. "This is kind of obsessive," JJ types.

"It's just a major muse mode," responds Benji, as he leans over to kiss Sara behind her ear.

More than Benji's girlfriend, Sara is the woman who helped all of us get over our shyness with and general distrust of white people. With Sara we learned many of her American customs, like hugging, and that took months of practice. "Arms out, touch face, squeeze!" We learn that Americans are able to take certain things for granted, like that the world appreciated their individuality. That they were raised thinking they were special, loved, and that their parents wanted them to follow their dreams and be happy. It was endlessly amazing.

We also learned English. We realized how different it really was to speak Chinese. We didn't used to have to say what we meant, because our old language allows for a certain amount of room to wiggle.

In Chinese we can ask, "What's it like?" because it can refer to anything going on, anything on your mind. The answer could be as simple-sounding as the one-syllable "men," which means, you're feeling stifled but lonely. The character drawn out is a heart trapped within a doorway. Fear is literally the feeling of whiteness. The word for "marriage" is the character of a woman and the character of fainting. How is English, that clumsy barking, ever going to compare?

But learn we did, useful acronyms like DTF (Down to Fuck), and Holy Shit, and we also became really good at ordering coffee. We learned how to throw the word *love* around, say "LOL" and laugh without laughing.

That afternoon, after coffee with Li Qiang, I buy her a parting present at an outdoor flea market. A *guoguo*, a pet katydid in a woven bamboo orb. They were traditionally companion pets for lonely old men, and the louder their voices, the more they were favored. Li Qiang picked out a mute one. The boy selling it to me says it lives for a hundred days.

"A hundred days?" she says as she brings the woven bamboo orb up against her big eyes. "This trapped little buddy is going to rhyme its own pitiful song for a hundred whole days?"

I tell her, "That's not so long, it's the length of autumn in Beijing. That's the length of a love affair." I realize I am giving away all my secrets. I think, *I want to roll you into the crook of my arm and take you somewhere far and green.* When she turns back toward me, I know the answer to my question before I even ask. I realize it is a mistake, the gesture, everything about me. She isn't going anywhere with me.

The only thing I have to offer her is money, and she has it already. I want to tell her that there's a lot of good shit about me that she would miss out on. But there's no art in me, and she sees it plainly in front of her. Instead, I kiss her fingers goodbye. They smell like cigarettes and nail polish, and I swear I'll never forget it.

By autumn, the trees shiver off their leaves and Zi Ying, too, becomes frigid and bored with Ah Ming. Our old friend Xiu Zhu comes back from "studying" abroad in Australia. She is a rich girl who looks like a rich boy. She has a crew cut, taped up breasts and a Porsche Cayenne, which she drives with one muscular arm on the steering wheel. Within an hour of meeting Zi Ying, we can all tell she is stealing her. By the time they finish their first cocktail, Xiu Zhu is already whispering English love songs into her ear.

We see less and less of Ah Ming after that. He still hangs out with the both of them, going to lesbian *lala* bars and getting himself hammered. The girls hold hands and laugh while he drinks whiskey after whiskey. He mournfully watches them kiss, as if he's witnessing an eclipse. Confused lesbians come up to him to ask where he got such a successful sex change operation, and he drinks until he passes out.

For my part, my father stops writing me e-mails asking about my well-being and just sends me a plane ticket. I don't tell anyone but I go to get my visa picture taken. The agency makes me take my earring out. Within the hour, the hole closes and now it's just a period of time manifested as a mole.

Winter, Zi Ying moves back to Hong Kong and breaks two hearts. Shortly after that, Ah Ming packs up his things as well. He tells us that under Beijing, beneath the web of shopping malls and housing complexes, lies the ruins of an ancient and desolate city. And beneath that there are two rivers, one that flows with politics and one that flows with art. If you drift here, you must quench your thirst with either of these waters, otherwise there is no way to sustain a life.

"I realize there is nothing for me here," he says, "no love here, not for a poor guy like me. It's waiting for me back in Xiamen, that's where it must be."

He sells his cameras, his clothes, even his phone.

"I don't want to leave a road to come back by," he says.

We all take Ah Ming to the train station, where he is leaving with the same grade-school backpack he arrived with. It's as if a spell has broken and suddenly we feel like jokers in our preripped jeans and purple Converses. We remember years ago, after having borrowed money from relatives, those first breaths taken inside that station. How timidly we walked forward with empty pockets and thin T-shirts. We had been *tu*, dirt, Chinese country bumpkins. And now one of us was giving up, but what could we have said to convince him he was wrong? What could have made him stay?

Everyone on the platform has their own confession to make, but when we open our mouths, the train comes, just in time to keep our shameful secrets, as trains are so good at doing. Someone is about to give away the mystery of loneliness, and then the train comes. The reason for living, the train comes, why she never loved him, the train comes, source of hope, train, lifetime of regret, train, never ending heartache, train, train, train, train, train.

Afterward, we huddle inside the station Starbucks, quietly sipping our macchiatos. Our cigarette butts are swept up by street sweepers whose weekly salaries probably amounted to what we paid for our coffee. The misty, mournful day is illuminated by the pollution, which makes Beijing's light pop, extending the slow orange days.

Out of nowhere JJ says, "I'm not sure if I actually like drinking coffee."

Sara says something about leaving soon to go home, and from the look on Benji's face, it is clear to me that this time, she might not be returning.

I want to say I might be leaving too, but instead I focus on an American couple sitting across the room from us. The woman holds in her arms a baby who doesn't look anything like her. They are an older couple, ruddy cheeked and healthy, and they order their organic juice and cappuccinos in English. As we sit together in those chairs, their Chinese baby starts screaming and banging his juice on the table. The couple is starting to look kind of despondent. The woman catches us staring, and the three of us look encouragingly at the baby. It's going to be OK, Chinese baby. You're a lucky boy. Such a lucky boy. Now please, please, shut up, before the Americans change their mind and give you back.

We somehow finish the Brass Donkey video and it's a semipornographic piece of garbage that gets banned immediately, of course. The band is happy because they're stamping "Banned in China" on their CDs and are being invited on a European tour. Without telling my friends, I go to the embassy to pick up my visa, secretly building the bridge on which to leave them. As I get out of there, I push back swarms of shabbily dressed Chinese people just trying to get a glimpse of America, and it makes me feel lightheaded with good fortune.

The crowded scene reminds me of waiting at the ferry docks when I was a little boy, before my father had any money, when my life was ordinary. Our region was very hilly and in order to get any kind of shopping done, we took ferries to reach the nearest mall. The rickety little boats were always so overcrowded and flimsy that they would regularly tip over into the river, spilling both the young and old into the river's green waters. What I remember most were these brief moments of ecstasy, when the small overloaded boat gave in and the water was met with high-pitched screams. And we'd all just swim to shore, laughing at our rotten luck. Everybody would then simply get on another boat, dripping with water, letting our wet clothes dry in the breeze.

Brass Donkey's now banned song is playing loudly in my head. It's really pretty good; it's actually a protest song hiding behind a disco beat. "We have passion, but do not know why. What are we fighting for? Where is our direction? Do you want to be an individual? Or a grain of sand."

EMERGING WRITER'S CONTEST WINNER
FICTION

In fiction, our winner is **Jasmine Sawers,** for her story, "The Culling."

Ploughshares fiction editor Margot Livesey writes: "From its opening paragraph, when the midwife sees a lantern flickering in the distance, 'The Culling' transported me. I admire the vivid use of detail, and I particularly admire how much the author omits, creating a sense that this unnamed country with its harsh customs really does exist. The story achieves a striking balance between the mythic and the  specific, the midwife is part of and partakes of both, and the result is an urgent and deeply satisfying reading experience."

Sawers is a native of western New York and attended Binghamton University. After teaching English in the Philippines, she says that she "came home and worked in retail, which is a never-ending source of material for those writers preoccupied with character." She is currently pursuing an MFA at Indiana University, and writes that she is "interested in the fairy tale and the place of the marginalized in America." Her work has also been published in *Art Voice* and *Construction.*

JASMINE SAWERS
The Culling

The night boasts the first edges of an autumnal chill. The midwife makes an acrid tea with her dried leaves; their dregs leave tremulous lines on the ceramic, like the mark of the tide on sand. She is swaying on her porch swing and staring out into the deepening black, the emptied mug clutched between her hands, when the light of a lantern begins to flicker half a mile away. The midwife straightens, and a cool calm overtakes her. This late, no one comes down her way, deep in the wilds, unless there is something wrong or a woman has gone into labor—and none of her expectant mothers are due for at least a month, three if they had done as told. The carpenter's wife could be septic from the abortion she got in the neighboring province—the midwife planned to chastise her after her recovery for taking her problem elsewhere. Or the seamstress could be having another miscarriage, or the berry picker's ill-planned first child could be early, or some father could have found his only daughter in a condition he wasn't expecting and didn't appreciate.

The screen door clatters against the slats of her cabin as she enters to collect her supplies. It's not enough to have clean cloths waiting in the linen closet—they must be as close to sterile as possible. Therefore, the midwife has developed a laundering schedule for her mountainous stacks of soft rags such that each is washed every three days, regardless of whether or not it has been put to use. This leaves her with her collection in thirds: one neat stack at the ready at any given moment; one soaking in a mixture of hot water, baking soda, and hydrogen peroxide; and the last in the process of drying on the line, outside in shafts of sunlight when weather permits. The midwife does laundry every day. She has rough, gnarled hands with skin like the tucktoo whose call echoes out from the corners of her cabin, the intruder she must chase out with a broom.

The floor of the linen closet is well stocked and orderly with supplies bought in bulk from the midwife's annual trips to a distant city: sterile gauze and strips of cotton cloth, sealed in plastic pack-ets; packages of unopened razor blades, right beside a single pair of blunt-tipped scissors for emergencies only; soft rubber suction bulbs, frequently boiled; antiseptic soap; a pocket-size scrub brush; bottles of sterile medical-grade alcohol; plastic bags; cotton balls; a small, power-ful flashlight and five packages of batteries; hemostats, also frequently boiled; box upon box of atraumatic needles with sutures, individually packaged; latex gloves; a stack of wide but shallow basins. Inert in the corner lies the midwife's sturdy canvas bag. When she is summoned, she can get everything she will require into that bag in forty-five seconds without even rushing.

She meets her visitor down the dirt path not five minutes after noticing him. It's the berry picker's husband, sweaty, watercolor face marked with a gray pallor even under the shadows of the lantern. He is panting, the curl of his breath hot on the midwife's skin as she stands too close, bag slung about one shoulder.

"It's too early," he tells her.

"Yes, obviously," the midwife says. "Tell me everything."

She sets a brisk pace even the berry picker's husband's long-legged stride cannot hope to match. The pregnancy had, until this point, been uneventful—the baby was prone to acrobatics, and could change position as many times as thrice in a single week, but it seemed to have settled into the proper downward orientation in the last fortnight. The berry picker had been experiencing what she thought was uncomfortable gas, her husband says, but the two of them had thought nothing of it until her waters burst, a warm, ominous flood in their sheets. It was at that point that her husband installed her in a warm bath and set off to fetch the midwife.

The fading residue of tear tracks on his face, glinting in the lamplight, does not move her, and she has no comforting nonsense sounds to make in his direction. She lets him ramble about each mean-ingless detail for the entirety of their trek back to the easterly village.

As they walk she thinks, in no particular order, of how a newborn's misshapen skull fills the palm of her hand; how to deliver a breech birth; how her aging heart and lungs protest the pace of her feet; how to light the furnace in her yard; how the soldiers raised the body of her daughter on a pike for all to see; how many seasons have passed since the current regime was installed; how many seasons have passed since she has touched someone outside the capacity of her vocation. How many seasons have passed.

"Do you think it will be a boy?" the husband asks after a whole minute has passed without his filling the silence. "You have ways of telling, don't you?"

"Do not presume upon me the ways of the Creator," the midwife says, and there is no more talk.

The berry picker and her husband live in a well-tended cabin on the outskirts of town with electricity and indoor plumbing—unlike some in the community, who are either too poor or too committed to the old ways, who still light gas lamps and make use of ramshackle outhouses erected on their properties by great-great grandparents. The husband holds some menial delivery job—milk or turnips or eggs; he's a bland man of many nerves, and the particulars of him slip like trifles from the midwife's mind.

The husband leads the midwife to the bathroom, where the berry picker sits hunched in the wide ceramic tub in the corner, naked and shivering over her belly. Long hair the color of dirty straw does not obscure how the knobs of her spine press taut against the skin of her back. She does not acknowledge the midwife when she enters and peers into the water—there is no blood.

The midwife slings off her coat before she addresses the husband: "Sheets, clean towels, blankets—every one you've got but for the one you'll sleep in next, and that rocking chair I saw on the porch. Bring it all to the bedroom. Quickly, man!"

The husband skitters out of the bathroom like a startled rabbit. The midwife sets her bag down, squats before the tub, and tips the berry picker's face toward her with an ungentle touch. "Have you been timing the contractions?"

"Twenty or so minutes apart still," she says. "I've done exactly as you said."

The midwife hasn't the energy to insist otherwise. It would be redundant anyway. She stands and plants her feet shoulder-width apart before extending her hands to the berry picker, palms up.

"Up you get," she says. "This tub is no place for a baby, or my knees." The berry picker grips her hands and the midwife pulls back, and together they haul the berry picker to her feet. She looks like many of the young women the midwife tends: slight and narrow but for the newly lush ponderousness of her breasts with their plum-flushed nipples and the swollen protuberance of her belly, bisected by the linea nigra. The mothers never eat enough, never gain enough weight, to satisfy the midwife. She lives in a state of perpetual disappointment.

The midwife yanks a towel from beside the sink and gives the berry picker a rough pat-down before leading her from the bathroom to the bedroom, where the husband is fussing with the arrangement of blankets on the mattress.

"You!" the midwife says, and he startles again. "Go get my bag."

While he complies, the midwife shakes out a blanket and places it on the wicker rocking chair, still cold from the night air. She gives the berry picker no choice, just eases her into the seat. The berry picker deflates with a relieved sigh as the chair rocks back under her weight.

The midwife tips the chair back and presses a foot into a rocker to immobilize it. She passes a hand over the berry picker's belly to feel the baby's rounded back—it's facing inward, as is proper. She presses three fingers of one hand just above the pelvic bone and three fingers of the other just beneath the diaphragm to palpate the womb: the baby is in the proper engaged position, its head nestled against the cervix. She will not have to encourage it to move lower with a firm, uncomfortable massage.

The husband returns and sets the canvas bag at the midwife's feet. With a quelling look, he is banished to the chair in the far corner of the room.

"Please let it be a boy," the berry picker whispers. "Please."

The midwife has learned to ignore the pleas of the mothers she tends, their fierce, often futile, wishes for sons. There is nothing she can do about what the Creator deposits into her arms, and there is nothing she can do about the laws of ignorant men. Once, such things set a fire in her empty belly, kept her up at night puking and shitting in peptic ire, but now, she is too old. She has no energy. Some say she has no heart.

Abruptly the berry picker keens and clutches at the arms of the rocking chair. Her distended belly lurches upward with the contraction, and she holds her breath.

"Keep breathing," the midwife says, "and don't push yet. It's not time."

"It *hurts*," the berry picker wails, as if the midwife doesn't know. As if the midwife hasn't been doing this for her entire life, hasn't given birth to her own child alone in her cabin, hasn't buried that child and learned what real pain is.

"Yes," is all she says.

Then the husband is hovering near the midwife's shoulder, his worry a thick, palpable thing that makes the air too heavy to breathe. The midwife wants to snap at him, to tell him to go back to his corner—men have never proven terribly useful during this portion of the proceedings. Instead, she tells him to go off to the side of the chair, to hold his wife's hand if he has to be here at all.

The contraction subsides, and the berry picker drops back into the chair, panting. The midwife removes her foot and lets the chair rock soothingly. The husband gazes down at the berry picker's slack face, brushing the fringe from her forehead and rubbing his thumb along the high ridge of her cheekbone. He bends to press his lips to her eyes, her temple. The midwife turns away to rummage in her bag.

She clears the bedside table and covers it with one of her fresh cloths. She arranges the remaining items in a neat line across the top. She doesn't turn back to the berry picker and her husband when she says, "You should walk around the room, get moving. Urinate and move your bowels, whether you think you have to or not. We should move to the bed when the contractions come quicker."

"Could it still be false labor?" The husband's voice, hopeful. "I mean—there's another month yet. Month and a half, even."

The midwife stares at her tools. Moves them minutely to be sure they're parallel. The metal ones shine under the bright electric lights. The berry picker knows what her body is bracing for—she has been the most attentive patient the midwife has attended in recent memory— and the midwife is weary of the business of soothing fretful men.

"Her waters have broken," she says. "Baby's coming now."

"And…and if it's a girl?"

"If it's a girl, I'll do what needs to be done."

The midwife sweeps from the room without a glance back at them, a basin and a bar of soap in hand. She fills the couple's tea kettle with water and waits for it to heat on their range.

Just before the water begins to boil, the midwife removes the kettle from the flame and pours it into a basin. She lathers the bar of soap and leaves it on the bottom; the skin of her hands does not protest the temperature, impervious. She cradles the basin in both hands carefully before bringing it back into the bedroom and placing it on the bedside table. The berry picker paces the length of the room with ginger steps, breath deep and measured, hands flexing at her sides. Her husband trails after her, broad hand pressed to the small of her back. He does not, at least, attempt to force conversation.

The midwife remembers when the berry picker was born: it was a bracing Thursday in late January some twenty-five years ago. The cord had been wrapped around her neck, but the midwife had been able to slip her fingers beneath its loop before her shoulders presented. The midwife used her hemostats to clamp the cord's blood flow, and she'd snapped at the father to be useful for once in his life and place his fingers where her own were keeping the child from choking to death. While he held the cord at bay, the midwife used one hand to support the head and the other to grope at her tools, which were so neatly organized that she got the blunt-tipped scissors in a single attempt. When the cord wilted between the hemostats, the midwife snipped the constriction away. The berry picker nonetheless remained stuck in place, her shoulders too cumbersome an obstacle to overcome without assistance. The midwife eased her head down until one shoulder popped out, then up for the other. With a strangled grunt from the mother, the berry picker slid out abruptly into the midwife's arms. Immediately the father crowded her to prize his child's legs apart, then turned stricken eyes upon the midwife.

"How many?" he asked. Just the previous week, the shepherd's wife had given birth to a girl, had gotten to keep her because the year's quota had not yet been met. She was the envy of her village—and the dark dread of every remaining pregnant woman.

"She's the third." The father exhaled, and the midwife turned away. "Tend to your wife," she said, and swaddled the baby in a clean cloth. The midwife bent to suck the mucous from the girl's nose, held her at a downward-facing angle, and finally the girl gave a gusty cry. The midwife handed her to the father, but could not bring herself to look at the grinning, sobbing mother, whose hands were outstretched for her prize. When the placenta was finally delivered—in infuriating pieces, delaying the midwife's departure—the midwife packed up her things and left without either new parent noticing.

When she was summoned again upon discovery of the mother's second pregnancy, the berry picker was three years old and followed her around the cabin like a duckling, asking incessant questions about the contents of her bag. Seven months later, in sweltering summer heat, the midwife snapped her newborn sister's neck, wrapped the little body in a plastic bag, and when she returned to her own cabin she incinerated it in the furnace the province installed in her backyard.

Now, hours pass as she watches the berry picker pacing, squatting, moving around to encourage labor, keeping hydrated. The time between contractions narrows. Finally, the berry picker kneels on the bed and rocks herself back and forth. She presses her face into the pillows, locks her body up, and moans as another contraction racks her, barely a minute after her last. Her husband rubs a hand over her back, and the midwife takes her place beside her.

"Stack the pillows," she tells the husband, "and we'll prop her up so I can check her progress."

They get the berry picker into position, and the husband stands as a sentinel beside her, her hand clutched in his. The midwife drags the bedside table to within arm's reach, snaps on a pair of gloves, and moves to kneel between the berry picker's spread legs. She slips two fingers inside the birth canal and presses gently against the cervix: the berry picker is just past nine centimeters.

"All right, girl," she says. "Pull your knees up and keep your breath steady, but don't push yet."

"Will it be soon?" the husband asks.

"It'll be when it'll be," the midwife says.

She turns to her array of tools and spills some rubbing alcohol on one of her smaller rags. She swabs over the berry picker's thighs, her vulva, her anus, before placing the rag into a plastic bag beside the bed.

"I just—I just need to know. If it's a girl."

When the midwife cranes her neck to meet his eyes, her teeth are bared in a snarl, and the husband quails against the wall.

"And if you'd followed my express instructions on when to conceive like everybody else, you wouldn't be in this position, wringing your fool hands. Stop speaking." It has been seven seasons since she's taken a life, and before that it had been twelve. With careful planning and common sense, the villagers can spare her that. They can spare themselves.

The berry picker's cries are hearty, guttural bellows, the rawest expressions of the world's most ancient pain. No high, girlish trills grate across the midwife's eardrums. There is strength here, and fear. Despite the tendril of unease that unfurls in her own gut, the midwife thinks of nothing but the measures of the berry picker's breath.

The berry picker's shouts go up an octave and a decibel, and the husband is whimpering under the crush of her hand around his, and the midwife is ready, ready. The raw pink slit of the berry picker's vagina spreads as the child's head pushes forward. The midwife can see dark locks of hair matted with blood and detritus.

"It's crowning!" she says. "Don't push, go slow. No one wants an episiotomy tonight."

The berry picker screams, the husband screams, her vagina stretches to obscene proportions, and then the head is out in the time it takes to draw a single breath. The berry picker slumps back into the pillows with a quavering wail, and her bowels void in a loose mess on the towel beneath her.

"Oh!" The husband looks queasy, though the berry picker seems unaware of what has transpired. The midwife sneers at him.

"It's nothing, happens all the time. This is why we have towels and blankets. Lift her and I'll get rid of it." Gingerly he moves to comply, but the midwife snaps at him. "Faster, you imbecile! We're ready to push!"

One-handed, the midwife rolls up the soiled towel and shoves it into the plastic bag. She turns back around, still supporting the head, and wipes at the berry picker's loins with another clean cloth, careful not to swipe upward. Afterward, she swirls her hand in the basin of soap and water. She leans in between the berry picker's upraised knees and meets wide, fearful eyes in a face flushed purple.

"You ready to push now?"

The berry picker nods and leans forward, hands tight around her knees. Her screams reverberate between the walls of the cabin as she bears down.

"All your strength, girl!" the midwife says. "All of it, now, now!"

The baby is small and it happens in a rush. With a final shout, the child is in the midwife's arms and the berry picker is trying to get a glimpse and the husband is coming too close. The midwife shrugs him off.

"You have to let me clean it first," she says.

"Just, please. Tell us."

The midwife sighs. She holds the child downward in the crook of her arm. "It's a girl," she says. "It's a girl."

She does not look up to see their expressions. The horror of it is dull for her, and those faces hold nothing new. The berry picker sags back with a defeated, mournful exhalation, and the husband begins to murmur unintelligible nonsense in her ear. The midwife wipes the child down and suctions out the fluid from its face, its lungs. It gives a resonant cry—it has healthy lungs, despite being born a month or more short of full term. She lays it down on the bed between herself and the berry picker. She takes off her soiled gloves and puts on new ones before plucking two strips of cotton from her spread of supplies. She waits for the umbilicus to stop pulsing fat and blue. When it withers and grows thin, she ties it off two and a half centimeters from the baby's navel. She unwraps a razor blade and slices through the cord between the two ties. She swaddles the baby and lifts it back into her arms.

"A little under two kilos, but healthy," she says. Around her heart, a fortress. "Do you want to see it?"

The husband's mouth quivers as he peers over the space between them to look at his daughter as if shy of her, but the berry picker squares her shoulders and holds out her arms. The midwife places the child where it belongs and is forced to endure the sight of the berry picker falling in love. Bile rises in her throat.

"Can't we hide her?" the berry picker asks, voice soft. The child latches to the proffered nipple with zealous expertise. "When the soldiers come?"

The parents of over-quota girl-children always ask this, as if the thought has never occurred to the midwife before. As if she hadn't tried that very thing decades ago, when the current regime and its population measures were new, as if she hadn't been punished beyond all imagining for it. *We are so remote in this province,* she'd thought. *How would anyone know?* Then, the militia came unannounced and flushed them out like vermin. All the children born that year and the year before in each of her villages were slaughtered by laughing men in navy uniforms, their bodies strewn on the streets for all to see and despair. The toddlers, the babies, and the midwife's own girl, old enough to sass and wield hemostats and know exactly what those soldiers were doing to her.

After the massacre, the midwife implemented her own program: in each of the five villages over which she presided, couples were to commune with one another on family planning, and only five couples per year were to conceive—always in April or May—in case every single child born was a female. This did not, of course, always go to plan. On buying trips to the city, however, the midwife had learned that her villages had a lower cull rate than many, and she was proud. Nonetheless, she had had occasion to determine the most humane means of committing infanticide, to perfect the flick of a wrist that would snap a newborn's neck in a fraction of a second.

"Won't do any good," the midwife says. "I'll palpate your stomach now."

The midwife realized long ago that it is better to take the child away as soon as possible after the birth. Lingering is a bittersweet torture the midwife cares not to indulge. She prefers the cleanliness of a quick departure—and the reprieve from hateful gazes is no small relief. She encourages delivery of the afterbirth by massaging the berry picker's belly, and when it comes, she catches it in an empty basin and stands with a creak of her bones. She moves to a lamp at the head of the bed and inspects it under the light: half a kilo, red, meaty, and full, it is thankfully complete, and the midwife's work is almost done here.

She drops the placenta into another plastic bag and checks the berry picker's passage for tears. The baby was so small, the midwife doesn't have to stitch anything up. She peels off her gloves and washes her hands in the soap and water before gathering her supplies to put back into her bag. She pulls out three sterile cloths and knots them securely into a sling that will hold the child tight against her body. When she approaches the family, she says nothing, merely holds out her arms. The husband begins to weep, shaking his head and begging, but the berry picker stills the progress of her tears and hardens her mouth. She dislodges the suckling child from her nipple, brushes a kiss across the downy forehead, and hands it to the midwife. The husband retreats into the bathroom with a slam of the door.

"It doesn't hurt?" the berry picker asks.

"It's over before it can," the midwife says. She is reasonably certain this is true—at least for one narrow version of the truth.

"We ask too much of you," the berry picker says. Her face is dry of tears, her mouth is free of tremors, her chin is high and proud.

The weight of the child in her arms suddenly makes the midwife feel very old and very tired. She passes the callused pad of her thumb over the hollow of the baby's throat to feel the hummingbird heartbeat. She pulls it close against her own bosom and breathes in its offal, iron smell—it hasn't yet been cleaned properly. The midwife bundles it more warmly and tucks it into the sling. The baby makes no fuss.

When the midwife leaves the cabin, her canvas bag is still inside. She will not go back for it. She will not be seen anywhere in these villages again.

The berry picker will know what to do.

EMERGING WRITER'S CONTEST WINNER
NONFICTION

In nonfiction, our winner is **Jacob Newberry**, for his essay "What You Will Do," about his experiences in Israel and Palestine.

The essay, *Ploughshares* editor-in-chief, Ladette Randolph, writes, "is the story of Newberry's own well-intentioned but misguided determination to resolve the differences between the Palestinians and Israelis (one shopping trip into Palestine at a time). It isn't easy to acknowledge our own failures of understanding and lack of sophistication in a complex world, and yet, if some part of the work of the essay

is to know oneself, Newberry has succeeded. This is a work of both beauty and humility."

Newberry is originally from the Mississippi coast, and is currently a PhD student in creative writing, with an emphasis on poetry, at Florida State University. He recently returned from Jerusalem, where he lived for a year on a Fulbright Fellowship.

"This essay," Newberry writes, "emerged from my naïve attempts to reconcile a whole series of complications that will probably never be solved. As a foreigner who chose to live in Jerusalem—where the conflict is difficult to ignore—I felt particularly challenged to 'do something,' despite being unable to determine what that might possibly be."

JACOB NEWBERRY
What You Will Do

Wake up while you are landing in Israel, the passengers all around you clapping. Smile when the older woman beside you clutches her purse, which you imagine holds a Bible. Be grateful that the flying is over. Take a shared taxi to Jerusalem. For a year this will be your home. Listen to Mahalia Jackson on your iPod—even though you are not religious—while you pass through the Judean hills, the city rising in the distance. She will sing "The Holy City" and it will be just as you had planned. You are a poet from Mississippi, and Jerusalem loomed throughout your vicious, strict, religious upbringing. You have been here, six years before, but entering Jerusalem will always seem important, symbolic. Go to the hostel where you will be staying until you find an apartment. You have been traveling for thirty-six hours and slept for approximately three of those, but it is 8 a.m. here. Keep yourself awake by any means necessary. You do not want to start your year with a bad sleeping schedule. Walk through the city—the warm, sunshine skies cheering you. When you are waiting for the light to change, close your eyes and begin to fall asleep. Keep walking. You will begin your year right.

Spend several weeks alone and unhappy, writing long letters to friends you love and miss. (This is one of your strange Victorian habits, writing letters by hand.) Fill them with melancholy and nostalgia; pepper them with verses from Isaiah and the Psalms, verses you learned in adolescence. Passages about Zion especially. Think often of Zion. Write of it obsessively. Assume it tires your friends, this topic, since you include something about it in every letter. Tell your friends in those long letters why it is important—report on it regularly, compare it to everything in the city. The bridge in the west, for example, which is designed to resemble David's harp. You will look at its suspension cables and believe fleetingly that they are iron threads in some great vessel's opening sail: you will believe that you have seen the Old Ship of Zion.

Remember songs you sang as a child. When finishing these letters, sing to yourself this line: *I've got a home in glory land that outshines the sun,* and by now it will be partly true: you will have found an apartment, looking out distantly on Zion.

Settle yourself in west Jerusalem. The few friends you have are in Tel Aviv—too far from you to see regularly, though close enough to prevent the ruinous emotional collapse that seems to be lurking very near. Life will be hard. You will spend your days in almost operatic sorrow: bleak, hopeless weeping in the mornings; sudden, irrefutable exhaustion in the afternoons. Above all, you will be lonely. And on some level you will feel a centerless spiritual sickness. This will manifest as physical sickness. This will worsen your despair. Your mother will say things on the phone to you like *You are protected in that city by God himself.* She believes this. On days when the cold is especially bitter, she will say *It must be the Lord's preferred climate, since that city is his residence.* In your weakened state you will almost forget that this is superstition.

But soon you will find friends. Your spirits will be lightened. You will be powerfully grateful. Still, the spiritual sickness will linger. You will not know its name, but you will feel it. You will love Israel on many levels and find it frustrating on many others. In this sense it will not be unlike America. But it will be an alien culture, and you will not try hard enough to love it, even though you know you should.

Go running. This is something you have loved for years. When the winds come up from Judea, when the clouds dissipate in the middle of the sky, when the cars have all passed and you have several moments of silence, you will be struck by a sensation like déjà vu; only it will not be déjà vu. With the white sun shining and your bright heart burning, you will for a moment believe that you have passed into the afterlife, that you are inhabiting already the New Jerusalem, that the Final Judgment has already come and gone. You will not be capable of verbalizing this experience except to recognize that in this moment, you are grateful you do not recall the hour of your own dying, whether it was painful or quick, whether you greeted it with determination or refused it with outrage. You will only know that you are grateful to have missed it. Then a taxi will speed through the curve without slowing, and so you will recall that you are alive. There is nothing you have missed.

On a day of particular sadness, go to Gethsemane with friends. Tell them the approximate age of the olive trees. They will not believe you. They will ask you to say it again. They will say *I'm going to Google this,* partly as a threat, but mostly in hopes that you know as much as you pretend, at least on this subject. After searching on their phones, you will be vindicated. You will walk toward the Catholic church at Gethsemane, the Church of All Nations; outside of it will be a sign in several languages that says *Please no explanations inside the church.* And so before going in, you will say to them: *I guess I'll give my explanations before we go inside the church.* They will listen carefully. You know the Bible and the history of Jerusalem much better than anyone you know. They each have a guidebook but prefer hearing it from you. While you are telling them of the stone inside the church where Christ prayed that night, of the agony, of the sweat that was maybe blood, of the famed request to *Let this cup pass from me,* the sound of centurions coming up the valley, the appearing of Judas in the midnight world, that famous kiss, in remembrance and in naming, you will wonder why it is, after these thousands of years, we all are still the same: come to a place despite our doubts, wanting to be told again what we already know. You will be confused that they prefer your telling to simply reading about it on their own, but you will accept it for what it is: their hearts, this day, belong to you. Treat this revelation with the reverence you imagine pilgrims have for the Garden itself. It is not so common a gift.

Go to Ramallah the next day. You will have already visited, but there is much to see. You will not have trouble entering Palestine; indeed, the small bus barely slows as it passes through the checkpoint. This is standard. It will seem promising, as though things are perhaps not so difficult as you have been told. Perhaps life is less unruly in its unfolding than the journalists and analysts and politicians claim. Perhaps, you will think, by coming regularly to Palestine (this is your fifth or sixth visit in a month), you are contributing, however meagerly, to bettering life on both sides. This is foolish but will not seem so at the time. You will reason: every time you visit, you spend money, which, though it perpetuates a great many inequities and stereotypes, is nonetheless demonstrably beneficial.

Strangers in the street will be eager to give you directions when you ask; they will often walk you to your destination, no matter the distance and inconvenience, smiling though they speak no English and you speak no Arabic. When you arrive, you will smile and say the single word you have learned: *Shukran.* Everyone will seem to be charmed. You will befriend the bank teller, who will take you and your friends for difficult-to-pronounce desserts that resemble orange Jello but which, he assures you, in halting English, are traditional and very delicious. When your friends tell him they live in Tel Aviv, he will not respond. And this is where you will believe you have begun to make a change, however small: because now he has met someone who lives in Tel Aviv and who is kind, even though you are all Americans and not actually Israelis. You will assume this is a first for him. It will seem like a start.

You will reenact this moment in mirrored reversal the next day, back in Jerusalem, with other friends who are Israeli, whom you had invited naïvely the previous day to also come to Palestine and who had reacted with bewildered astonishment. *Of course I can't go,* one of these friends had told you. *I'm a Jew.* This will have seemed impossibly over-simplified but will soon become axiomatic. But before it does, you will still be hoping to effect only the smallest of changes, aiming, you hope, for an achievable goal: telling stories is something that can make a dif-ference. You will be proud of yourself for maintaining idealism without veering into naïve foolishness or neocolonialism. You are only telling stories, after all, and their effect will be small, but that (you will reason) is at the heart of why it just might work; this is how real change hap-pens. So you will tell your Israeli friends, whom you love and who are beautiful and kind, of your day in Ramallah. *We met the nicest guy,* you will say. *We were a bit worried to say my friends lived in Tel Aviv, but he didn't care at all.* Wait for the impact of this statement on your Israeli friends. *Small changes,* you will think. *All they want,* your friend will say, *is for us to die.* Disagree with this. Assume you are well traveled and erudite and sophisticated and very well informed. Say something like *All they want is to live their lives in peace, just like you.* Try not to be offended when the look on your friend's face resembles a parent's. You are good friends; there is room for disagreement without hurt feelings or dismissal. But you have been rebuffed. Even your smallest dose of optimism has been undone.

You will go to bed that night deflated and surprised by your own naïveté. Did you really think you could make an appreciable change in the world's most celebrated conflict, in a single day, no less? Is it just as condescending and unjustifiable as it now seems, to come in from America, and after three months believe you can and should try to make a difference? But this will be the central question for you, then: what are you supposed to do, and why are you always anxious, always sick? You will think of the people you have met who have lived here for many years, all of whom seem to be terminally indifferent: there is no room, they say, for any change; everything is stagnant. You will wonder if this state of despair (if it is despair) is normal, or inevitable, or if there is another way.

Realize, then, in bed and unable to sleep, that this is the central concern: how to maintain optimism and enthusiasm despite an arraying gallery of failures. This is the heart of your spiritual sickness: your impotence versus your earnestness, both of which are compelling, along with the existential dread that is impossible to shake. You have made no difference, and you will make no difference, and in the end this is precisely what was expected. The only question is to what extent the experience will have disillusioned you. Understand, then, that there are two options (even though this is not true): foolish idealism or cynical defeatism. You are too old, you will reason, and too proud of your own sophistication and intelligence, to fall victim to the first. But you will not be old enough, not sufficiently jaded, to fall victim to the second. There should be another way. Go to sleep. It has been a long day.

Go running the next day. You will still be carrying a great many things with you. Remember how peaceful life can be, as you climb the hills outside Jerusalem, as you silence the music in your headphones when the hill crests and the mountains shine in the haze, green and resplendent. Be grateful for the dark soil that smells of home, just beside the trail. Touch it. Admire the rich brown of your stained fingers. Think of how beautiful life can sometimes be. Be grateful that at least there is beauty and tranquility and simplicity in the natural world.

Be grateful, in this moment, for simplicity. When a car drives noisily past, the moment will be gone. Try to recapture it when it drives away. Say the word out loud: *simplicity*. And then try not to totter over as this word collapses in your mouth. There is no simplicity, no tranquility, without complication.

You are running in the prosperous western side of Jerusalem, which no Palestinians can visit. It feels like any western European city, if sunnier. You are safe to wander in the afternoons and evenings, free to do as you please. The dominant aesthetic is from the Western world, which is why you can occasionally feel at home. You will be struck just then with an unshakable feeling of complicity: with the Occupation, with the whitewashing of conflict, with the culture of triumphant militarism. But this will be too reductionist. There are so many elements, so many historical and cultural considerations that cannot be simply explained away. You will begin to feel dizzy. You will wish you were living at home again, in America, where things are simple. Life is easier there. Familiar. The web of inequities is not so far reaching. There is no systematized exploitation, no history of racial oppression. But this retreat, of course, will quickly fail. Your own privilege and wealth at home are only invisible to you. They have been all along. This recognition will make you dizzier. The layers of complicity in your life in America—with racial and economic injustice, with robber capitalism, with the blind destruction of the natural world, with militarism and empire—are so deeply folded into your life as to be unidentifiable. Close your eyes and breathe. Remind yourself to breathe again.

Run home. Your apartment is in Rehavia, a quiet neighborhood full of wealthy retirees. Since you are neither wealthy nor retired, your apartment is a dump, but it is, at least, a home. (It will continue to be your habit, as you like to say, of living in the dumpiest apartment in the nicest part of town, whatever city you are living in.) Take a shower. You deserve this. At least this is simple, you will say to yourself. Pure physicality. Hot water and a heated room and a cold drink. Your glass of ice water will look beautiful on the counter, perspiring silently in the hot room. Clear your mind. Soreness and endorphins. Relief. Simplicity.

But it will start again, even as you begin to relax: that unflagging doubt. Maybe this house was formerly occupied by Palestinians, before the Nakba. Maybe its inhabitants were forced into refugee camps in the panic of 1948. You will have no way of knowing. Maybe, even though you are of neither Jewish nor Arab ancestry, you are perpetuating a grave injustice just by living here. But this is too reductionist, again. Nothing is so simple as that. Israel is beautiful. You do not disagree with Zionism, only certain elements of its implementation. The Israelis you know are kind and friendly and endlessly interested in visiting America, which you find a continually endearing trait. And who are you to judge the implementation of Zionism? You are not an expert in geopolitical conflict, nor are you steeped in the history of the region. You are just a poet from Mississippi who has always dreamed of living near Golgotha, a twentysomething on leave from your PhD studies to write lyric sonnets recounting the songs that pilgrims sing in unison as they amble across the tiled floor near Christ's grave. You are not a politician or an analyst or a strategist; indeed, you will sometimes spend an entire evening thinking only about the color of the city's walls at dusk, glowing pale sienna in the failing sun, wondering if the shade was the same when Isaiah looked over Jerusalem and declared: *How lovely on the mountains are the feet of him who brings good news, who announces peace and brings good news of happiness, who announces salvation.* There is no need, you will say to yourself, to be so conflicted. Just find a way to be happy. Just find a way to accept the great pleasure of a hot shower.

Now turn the water off. You have been in there too long. This is wasteful, and water in this country is in short supply. In fact, some people fear a war over resources will break out soon. Do not contribute to the coming war with your wastefulness.

A few weeks later, go again to Ramallah. You will have worked out, to some extent, the location of your discontent, but you will not have determined how to quiet it. In conversations with friends, in long letters, in feverish e-mails, you will have discerned some of the rationale behind these visits to Ramallah. Always with a friend. Usually with a specific purchase in mind. Tell yourself that spending money in Palestine is actually beneficial, both to the local economy and to the morale of the people living there. Do not give in to the rather pressing counterarguments about the bleakness of consumerism as a political tool. Say to yourself what you have said in muted exasperation to your friends back home: *What, am I supposed to solve the Middle East?* This is not your war. These are not your people. This is not your country. Even the number of international aid workers and volunteers living and working in Ramallah will satisfy and dismay you: there are others here already, better equipped and more determined to make a difference than you, so you need not feel so superfluous. Their concern is genuine, and some of them are very effective. Others, though, seem to be here only for the mystique of living beside a conflict they have long heard about. They will be easy to recognize, talking loudly on the bus in English, no matter their country of origin, saying things like *I think everyone should live in Palestine at least once in their lives.* You will nod politely and they will continue. *What I'm doing here just feels so vital.* They will make you want to disavow any altruistic impulse, if only to avoid sounding so obnoxious. But they are young, you will say to yourself, magnanimously. They have not yet acquired your superior mix of optimism and worldliness. Take pride in your own silence and dignity.

This time, as every time, going into Ramallah will be easy. You will buy a decently constructed pair of shoes from a very nice shop run by a friendly man who remembers you and your tall, handsome friend. The shoes will say *Handmade in Palestine,* in English, on the hard black soles. This is not the only reason you have purchased these shoes (think: upward mobility, redistribution of wealth, joblessness), but it is a selling point. The owner of the shop knows this. His shoes are more expensive than those at most stores in the city, and each time you have come to visit, only foreigners have been browsing. Smile when you recognize the shop owner's cleverness. Feel it warmly as a reverse exploitation, one that benefits everyone. Think of the phrases *monetizing the conflict* and *exploiting Western liberal guilt* and be proud of your erudition and sophistication. The other shoppers have probably not figured out why they want these shoes precisely, but you have. Your degree of self-awareness is admirable; it is further reason to feel proud. You will imagine then how to naturally fit into a conversation, once you have moved back to America, that these shoes were handmade in

Palestine. Saying it openly would backfire, would seem boastful and indulgent, would have very much the opposite of the desired effect. You will think of ways to let it occur naturally. People sometimes ask where a person has gotten his shoes from. Someone might find them beautiful and inquire. But often they do not. What might work better is to stop one night, while walking home from a bar with friends whose approval you seek, to retie the shoes, whether needed or not. This will subtly bring attention to them, and someone might then ask *Where did you get your shoes?* Then you will be able to reply, quite casually, *Oh, I bought these in Ramallah* and await the admiration that will come as a result. If you are feeling particularly chatty, you will be able to then talk about reverse exploitation and monetizing the conflict and Western liberal guilt and consumerism as a crass but effective weapon against economic and political stagnation, and you will then have the opportunity to feel erudite and meritorious. It will make a good impression. And the shoes are also beautiful. Everyone wins.

You will think of all of this while you are handing the shopkeeper your money. Satisfaction, if not simplicity, all around.

Then it will be time to leave Ramallah. You will take a bus for four shekels to the Qalandia checkpoint, the main way to cross the Wall and head back to Jerusalem. Once—on your first visit—you stayed on the bus once you reached the checkpoint, with three friends, even though the only other people remaining on the bus were either very old or carrying a baby. When the soldiers came onto the bus to search for weapons and explosives, the four of you continued chatting amiably, until one of the soldiers asked for your passports. Two of you had forgotten them, but as you were all Americans, all young, all smiling and friendly and attractive, the soldier only said: *Try to remember your passports next time.* He smiled, then added: *And you're usually supposed to get off the bus and walk through the checkpoint.* Since then you have tried on each occasion to make this happen again.

So, then: stay on the bus, even though almost everyone else has gotten off. This time the soldier will be a woman, and she will be unforgiving. *You need to walk through the checkpoint like everyone else,* she will tell you. Do not sigh audibly; this will aggravate her. Because you have waited so long to get off the bus, the line at the checkpoint now is lengthy. Stand together, the two of you, holding your newly purchased shoes in a bag that has *Handmade in Palestine* printed in red lettering on the side, standing near the end of the line beside an experienced crowd of mostly women. Everyone will be annoyed by the situation, but you will be especially so. Say to your friend, out of weariness and an instinct to respond to stress with humor: *What good is Western privilege if we still have to wait in this line?* It will seem very clever. But you will both be quite annoyed. There are friends waiting for you in Jerusalem and the process is taking a very long time. What will be worse is your knowledge that this is only the first of three levels of security before passing through to the other side of the Wall.

You will all be crowding toward a revolving door made of iron bars; they will look precisely like prison bars you have seen on TV. The bars will be painted blue. The door will be controlled by an electronic system with hydraulics that you will not pretend to understand. Above it will be a large, ominous camera and two lights, red and green. The door will be locked and thus not revolving, the red light illuminated. Far ahead of you, standing in front of what soon will be the opening, will be an old woman with a green headscarf who is holding many bags, poised to hurry through once the light turns green and the loud clamor begins as the door starts its mechanical wheeling. You will be moving closer, but the process is very slow. Only three people, on average, will make it through the door before the buzzing stops and the loud hammer of metal on metal strikes again. The red light will be illuminated. The camera will be turning quietly from side to side. You will be standing next to a woman in her early thirties. She will have her ID card out and ready, but you will not be able to make out her name. It is in Arabic, in any case, which you do not read. You will have made little progress in thirty minutes. The damp wind makes it very cold. You will resolve not to come often to Ramallah anymore.

At last you will make it through the revolving metal door. Now you will take off your coat and empty your pockets. Place your bag on the conveyor belt. Walk through the metal detector. Once the bag has been cleared, you will turn to two soldiers, who are reclining in front of glowing monitors, warm behind several impenetrable inches of glass, and show them your American passport. The people who pass through every day will raise theirs to the window, folded open already to the photo page. You, however, will make a small show of revealing the gold eagle against the deep blue of the leather cover, the elegant lettering that says *United States of America*. The soldiers will be happy to see this. They will pay little attention to the photo page. They will wave you through quickly then, and you will say to your friend (who has done the same as you): *At least they know a good thing when they see it,* and you will both laugh, take your bags, and move quickly past the old woman with the green headscarf, the one with the many bags, the one who was far ahead of you in that long-ago line behind the blue iron revolving door, whose bags are now spread out on a wide black metal table, being meticulously picked through by a teenaged soldier in a dark olive uniform, with a large machine gun on his shoulder. She will be standing several paces back from the table, her hands left limply at her sides, her eyes downcast, waiting in weariness and dejection. As you walk past her, you will stop laughing. She will not have noticed you.

There is one more layer of security: another soldier behind very thick glass. He will also see your passport and smile. *Welcome to Israel,* he will say to you, and you will be happy. Once through, you will turn to your friend and say *That was the worst* and he will agree. You will both shake your heads and imagine what the experience must be like for people who go through this every day, like the old woman with the green headscarf and the many bags. *I can't imagine,* you will say to each other, quite truthfully. This comment will seem to you magnanimous and large of spirit. This consideration will allow you to disregard your unmanageable guilt, the futile wrestling over your substantial privilege, the purposelessness of your displeasure in the middle of it all. It will feel as though you deserve to exercise this privilege maybe a bit more than the kind of Americans who might go through and not empathize with the old woman with the green headscarf and the many bags. And besides, you will reason, this state of affairs was not created by you, nor can it be changed by you alone. Your awareness of it, then, will seem particularly admirable. This, again, will help to alleviate your guilt.

That night, after meeting your friends, after walking freely throughout the city, after telling them how *impossible* the journey back was, you will go home, and the old dread will resurface. The hard-to-define spiritual sickness. *Just go to sleep,* you will tell yourself. It has been a very long day.

The next day, go to Tel Aviv, where you will sit by the windy sea and write a letter filled with longing to someone you love perhaps more than anyone in the world. You write to her often. You will be deeply moved: the water, rising and falling in familiar, unhurried regularity. You will be seated on a bench and it will be windier than you like, but this brings to you the scent of salt in the air and reminds you of home. There will be families that walk by you in the early evening, joggers that rush past in the remaining sunlight, strangers that quiet their blanched mourning for a moment to watch the sea and the lingering star behind. You will all be engaged in an act of benediction: of fellowship with the natural world in its full-throated splendor. It will be miraculous.

You will be overcome by the sea: looking out while the sun declines into the waiting green field of salt and foam, this element of creation seeming to surpass the others. And there will be creatures living splendid and unaffected beside you, hurtling outward in the sweet perpetuity of their only lives. You will write in your letter, and it will feel like healing: *I see a gathering of sea birds, descending in their riotous way, to one portion of the ocean's inconstant surface, to descend, descend, into the very current of another world.* You will wish then that you were one of them, that your life were so simple, every moment of it having transpired beside the sea. It will be a blessing, this wish. It will be an answer of some kind.

And so you will not allow yourself to think, just then, that only fifty miles south of you, in a place you will never be able to reach, there may be a poet on the beach in Gaza, looking out at the same transcendent sea, wishing something very similar.

EMERGING WRITER'S CONTEST WINNER
POETRY

In poetry, our winner is **Jen Silverman,** for her series of Bath poems.

Ploughshares poetry editor John Skoyles writes: "Silverman's poems have a declarative force and a surprise in every phrase, a combination that results in a tone both intimate and astonishing."

Silverman is a New York–based poet and playwright who has, so far, mainly received attention for her work in the theater. Her full-length play *Crane Story* premiered off-Broadway in 2011 with The Playwrights Realm, and her one-act, *The Education of Macoloco,* won the 2009 Samuel French Off Off Broadway Festival. She is currently working on her first book of poems. The Bath series in *Ploughshares* is her first poetry publication.

"I'm fascinated by bathing as a ritual and ceremonial act as much as a sensuous one," Silverman writes. "As someone who has studied martial arts on and off since childhood, I heard again and again that good martial artists move like water—with grace, malleable and adaptable, claiming nothing, tied to nothing, but capable of great concentrated force. Particularly given my own nomadic upbringing, I'm fascinated by a narrator who moves like water through a world of encounters that, even as they slide away, leave a lasting mark on her."

Bath 3 (Iowa City)

That winter a fever came
and didn't depart till spring
everything happened through a curtain

the bills the rent the love affairs with men
I couldn't keep separate in my mind
I'd never liked blonds

but they were so bright they caught my eye
like lucky coins I plucked them up and
there you go next thing you don't know

one from the other and blame it on the fever but
the sensitive ones will leave your bed and go
out into the cold, hearts bruised, and what can you do

I went back to bed that winter
I ran baths late at night then didn't undress
sat at the edge of the tub and watched the water

quiver like a fugitive, I don't remember that I
ever saw my reflection
in the spring the fever left

everything was clear-edged and merciless
and I picked my lovers for their black hair
and their black black eyes

Bath 4 (Kentucky)

They dropped you in the river. They said
Praise Jesus, Praise Him. You bobbed up

half drowned. You had seen clearly from
the bottom. Through the silt. Somewhere in

the river mud, you lost your God. So here
we are. And your long bones are light.

You are no longer tethered to this world.
You have un-believed yourself into liberty.

It does not feel like victory, you say,
to go from believing everything to nothing.

You doubt the reality of the sun, the wine,
your own long fingers, the rich moss, ice.

You return to water. Always, the water's edge.
And I trail after, afraid you'll stumble in,

reel yourself back to the bottom, back to a
reckoning, your face against the silt, your fingers

combing through riverweed. I run you a bath.
I step into it in your stead. I lie at the

bottom, staring up through clear water, toward
the windows. I see nothing,

I see nothing but light.

JEN SILVERMAN
Bath 5 (New Hampshire)

If it's one drink, it will be two. Wisteria tangling
around your wrists. Here is where you buried your

father. Here is where you buried your brother.
Here is where they will bury you, when the

time comes. No wonder you drink yourself down
toward the earth. Home is where the shovels lie.

Earth and earth and earth. Stones crowd your sleep.
Granite and salt, sand giving birth to

the fortress where even your lovers sigh. Silent
underfoot. You dream yourself toward them.

You are foxfire, you are phosphorescent. Your
mouth like whiskey. Your eyes like whiskey.

You baptize yourself in sorrow, again and again.
You baptize yourself with bourbon and brandy.

You swim downward, fast salmon, heedless, handsome,
death is in you, it has captured your ear. You have your

father's jaw, your brother's chin. When you were born
they bathed your small body with their fears.

Each scar they'd earned became manifest on your skin.
Their love aches like a badly set bone. When the river takes

you, it will be no new baptism. Just that same, ancient sacrifice.
Just that rush, that rushing, and then you are gone.

Ladette Randolph is editor-in-chief of *Ploughshares* and the author of three books of fiction: two novels—*Haven's Wake* (forthcoming  from University of Nebraska Press, spring 2013) and the award-winning *A Sandhills Ballad* (University of New Mexico Press, 2009)—and the short story collection *This Is Not the Tropics* (University of Wisconsin Press, 2005). Randolph is on the faculty of the Writing, Literature, and Publishing department at Emerson College in Boston. Prior to joining the staff at *Ploughshares* she was an acquiring editor and associate director at University of Nebraska Press. She is the recipient of a Pushcart Prize, a Rona Jaffe grant, the Virginia Faulkner Award, a Best New American Voices citation, and four Nebraska Book Awards.

John Skoyles has published four books of poems, *A Little Faith* (1981); *Permanent Change* (1991); *Definition of the Soul* (1998), and

The Situation (2007), all from Carnegie Mellon. His work has appeared in *Poetry, The American Poetry Review, The Atlantic, Harvard Review, Slate, Yale Review,* and *The* Poetry *Anthology, 1912-2002,* among others. He is also the author of a collection of personal essays, *Generous Strangers* (Kodansha International, 1999), and a memoir, *Secret Frequencies: A New York Education* (University of Nebraska Press, 2003). His awards include grants from the National Endowment for the Arts, as well as fellowships from the New York and North Carolina Arts Councils.

A LIFE IN A HOUSE

A Plan B Essay by Timothy Schaffert

*In the Plan B essay series, writers discuss their contingency plans,
extraliterary passions, and the roads not traveled.*

I've been pushed from my own rooms by my own things. I now live in
the belfry, batty as a spinster aunt, with just a little circle of stained glass
as my window out. I pick petals and blooms from my own garden for
tea, bind them with leaves, and leave them to dry in the rusted birdcage
that the canary escaped. Needles from the heart of the coneflower. Pearls
of jasmine. Rosebuds and cloves. In winter, I add ginger and garlic to
fend off colds and flus. Sipping hibiscus water lessens the pressure of the
blood in the head (which is to say, it files the edges off your headaches).

The attic window's on a hinge, and that's how I look out. I oversee
a cemetery. I am its only survivor. There is no caretaker, other than
me, but I find I like it overrun and overtaken with noxious weeds and
prairie grasses. I'm happy to see the limestone crumble and lean. Every
morning, I sip tea and take mental note of the cemetery's latest decline.
The Russian thistle is uncivilized.

I'm very careful on the stairs, as each step is stacked with old
magazines and newspapers. The hazard is increased by my habit to
read on the way down. Yesterday morning, a nineteenth-century
cyclone killed a family of twelve. The day before that, an old woman in
1974 was taken in by thieves who sold her a false bill of goods. I find
catastrophe and hoax at every step of my morning descent.

You're probably wondering: *But what is the strangest thing about
him?* The strangest thing is likely that I live among many broken
objects despite the fact that I'm not sure I've ever broken anything
in my life. Not a dish, not a nose. I'm not in any way addle-fingered,
and I've never been. If anyone who has ever known me can think of
anything I've ever broken, I wish you'd tell me, because I have myself
convinced that I'm peculiarly (perhaps magically) not-clumsy.

I sell my things to folks who happen by, or I buy the things they want to sell me. I once bought from someone a sign that says *We Buy and Sell Antiques,* and I set it on my porch, and that was that. If you haven't gathered as much, I live in the country, but I do have cousins who live in the city. Whenever I go to the city, my cousins have a party, and they insist I dress like an eccentric. They invite different people to each party so that I can tell the same stories over and over. They love to introduce me. Last time, I wore a red silk kimono patterned with cowboys on bucking broncos. I wore a tuxedo shirt with a ruffle and the trousers from a seersucker suit. I wore the type of hat they used to call a trilby, and maybe they still do. My cousins' friends are all young and sophisticated in that stupid way, and they admire me because I'm nothing they would ever want to be, despite the things they say: *Your cousin has the most remarkable life. What a dream that would be. Can you imagine just hiding in the country to hoard? I wish I could be so pleased with such simple pleasure.* These boys and girls wear clothes too small for them—trousers that don't reach to their ankles and dresses that don't reach their knees. They wear T-shirts that rise up when they laugh and preen, revealing belly buttons that seem so frequently to be outies, as if the outie is infinitely more fashionable than the innie.

I spend my days fixing my broken things, though I don't have a mind wired for mechanics. I converted a Louis Quatorze–style sideboard into a workbench, and I stand at it until daylight's gone. I putter. I wear a pair of reading spectacles, and another pair in front of that pair, and another pair in front of that, to magnify. I repair the tinny notes of music boxes. I polish the blind eyes of china dolls. I restring marionettes, patch the tires of toy cars, correct the lenses of complicated cameras, and comb the fleas from the mange of taxidermied lapdogs. I take my lunch in the conservatory, where I've parked a candy-apple-red Chevrolet Bel Air. I sit in the car with a thermos of coffee and a sandwich of shaved beef tongue and pickles I pickled myself. I look in the rearview mirror and practice the best way to smoke my French cigarettes.

In the early falls and late springs, I spend many evenings on the stage of the community theater in the little town up the way. The theater is a restored opera house in the upstairs of a hardware store. Sarah Bernhardt once performed there when her train was stalled by a blizzard. With nowhere to go, she and her troupe slapped together a truncated version of Ibsen's *The Lady from the Sea*. In the lobby, under glass, is a boot of pale-blue damask and buttons of pearl believed to have been worn by Bernhardt on stage. I once played Bernhardt in a play I wrote myself: *I, the Actress Sarah Bernhardt*. In my play, I play Bernhardt playing Hamlet.

I play many roles, whether men or women. There aren't many actors or actresses in town, so I have my pick of all the greatest characters. I play demons as effectively as I play angels, slipping beneath the skin of the most skin-crawlingly vicious, or bringing a touch of divinity to cherubs and heroines. My Peter Pan was so honest I made the children cry. I gave everyone the willies with my Blanche DuBois. I played each and every character in a one-man production of *Our Town*, and won a certificate from the county chapter of Job's Daughters.

There are probably those who grow weary of seeing me in every play, but our audiences are far too polite to criticize. Even the paper's critic never judges. She neither raves nor rants. She simply describes. She attends each performance, then returns to her desk after dark, in the locked newspaper offices, to file her review before midnight, a review which is, without fail, a simple outline of plot and listing of the cast members.

We do three plays per season, two weekends per play. We sell more tickets than we have seats. We've never not been blessed with a standing ovation. The florist brings me roses. The librarian has me autograph the playbill for the archives.

I go home abuzz, my whole body electric, as if I'd knocked my funny bone and sent a ringing through every inch of my skeleton. I drink brandy from my lucky teacup, a china cup from the set of a woman who sunk with the Lusitania. And my very high high plummets to a very low low, and I'm up all night, restless, running through my mind the details of all the other lives I should be living.

Timothy Schaffert's novel The Swan Gondola, *a story of love and ghosts set among the flimflam men, snake-oil salesmen, occultists, and actresses of the 1898 Omaha World's Fair, is forthcoming from Riverhead/Penguin. Schaffert is the author of four other novels, all from Unbridled Books:*

The Phantom Limbs of the Rollow Sisters, The Singing and Dancing Daughters of God, Devils in the Sugar Shop, *and* The Coffins of Little Hope. *His work has been a Barnes & Noble Discover New Writers selection, an Indie Next pick, and a* New York Times Book Review Editors' Choice. *He teaches in the English Department at the University of Nebraska-Lincoln, is the director/founder of the (downtown) Omaha Lit Fest, and is a contributing editor to* Fairy Tale Review.

A Look2 Essay on Jaimy Gordon by John Domini

The Look2 essay series, which replaces our print book reviews, takes a closer look at the careers of accomplished authors who have yet to receive the full appreciation that their work deserves. Reviews of new books can still be found on our blog at http://blog.pshares.org/

If literature were politics, Jaimy Gordon would be the victim of a cabal. When she took home the 2010 National Book Award for her racetrack novel *Lord of Misrule,* the larger literary forums blinked at the news, astounded. At *The New York Times*—the daily, not the Sunday *Book Review*—Janet Maslin didn't resist the cliché "bolt from the blue." Maslin did go on to praise *Misrule,* calling it "assured, exotic," and "an incontrovertible winner," but her review also got off a sneering parenthesis about the shoestring publishing house, McPherson & Co. Overall, the effect was rather a backhanded compliment. The novel came off like a hothouse flower, lovely but out of the way, for special tastes only. Indeed, Gordon's books have yet to draw notice in the *Sunday Book Review* or *The New York Review of Books,* among many other places, and if literature were politics, there could be no denying how this woman's been shunned. Her name has never been linked to that of some Manhattan angel. For decades she's taught in the hinterlands of Kalamazoo, and she's published little journalism or criticism, those bite-size pieces of sensibility that can cause readers to hunt for more.

Indeed, this author has been slow to produce anything. *Misrule* is only her fourth novel since 1974. A couple of experimental dramatic pieces, which the author calls masques, can be tracked down. Other-wise, the most notable works are a pair of historical narratives, one a farce about Civil War Reconstruction, *Circumspections from an Equestrian Statue* (1979), and the other a free-verse fantasia of Prohibition bootlegging that features, of all people, Gordon herself: *The Bend, the Lip, the Kid* (1978). Their experimental qualities include brevity;

together, these works run less than 150 pages.

Yet it does this writer a disservice to measure her accomplishment the way Andy Warhol would, ignoring the substance and measuring the inches. Neglect is endemic among serious authors, and Gordon's done better than some. She's enjoyed attention in magazines such as *Gargoyle* and *Context,* and she's raked in a starry array of blurbs from writers as diverse as Gilbert Sorrentino and Jayne Anne Phillips. She's won other awards, major grants, and inclusion in *Best American Short Stories* (the piece introduced characters later in *Misrule*). Her 1990 novel, *She Drove Without Stopping* (Algonquin), was named a Notable Book by the American Library Association, and in 2000 *Bogeywoman* (Sun & Moon) made a similar short list at the *Los Angeles Times.* These two will get a close look here, along with the title that's made the woman famous, or sort of famous—and the point is, fame and its vagaries can't be the primary criterion in assessing what she's accomplished.

Without Stopping, Bogeywoman, and *Misrule* have more durable qualities. Their style alone achieves rare enchantment and risk, even in an incidental description, like "cowbells bouncing down a glass staircase, that was her laughter" (an aside in *Bogeywoman*). Brief passages cast such a spell they can cloud the seriousness of the larger project, a coming of age without end.

The young women at the center of Gordon's full-length narratives struggle within the rubbery confines of the white American middle class. All three have Jewish roots, and this has a bit to do with their inability to accept, to settle. Their more profound unease, however, stems from their bourgeois conditioning, not to say cushioning. Each starts out a well-off, well-educated Baltimore girl—the protagonists of *Bogeywoman* and *Lord of Misrule* are sisters—and they're more than smart enough to see they have advantages denied many others. They never fail to notice, in their roughly Southern environs, the more limited resources of the nearby African Americans, leading a dray or pushing a broom. Yet the girls end up betrayed by their intelligence and privilege. When they forage beyond its limits, in the hallowed pursuit of happiness, they blunder into the school of hard knocks. Though each girl makes it into her twenties, she's lucky to get that far. While the novels must be considered comedies—that's the only word for them—each turns a Suburban Suzy into a creature of myth. She faces down monsters, but achieves nothing you'd mistake for the American dream.

Gordon hit this stride in 1990, with *She Drove Without Stopping*. Her lone novel before that is something else again, a boy's initiation, in an alternative universe. The eponymous fledgling in *Shamp of the City-Solo* (1974, reissued on McPherson in '93) shrugs off his stultifying hometown of "Bulimy" (ring a bell?) and takes on a more challenging dystopia, Big Yolk, the "City-Solo." There, following as best he can the lessons of masters like the "Topical Tropist" Sergei Shipoff, the teenage Shamp finds his calling as a kind of performance poet. Shipoff ships Shamp off (to employ a fitting tongue twister) as a "novice lector." The apprentice scuttles down Caligari byways, sits through nuthouse oratory, and finally takes the podium, speechifying with his life on the line at the "Arslevering Ox Roast." In this citywide competition, literally do-or-die, Shamp emerges victorious.

His reward reveals something about the game afoot, in that it recalls that other surrogate cityscape, Monopoly. The winning "soloist" at the Roast is given a great hotel in a posh district. Boardwalk or Park Place, one wonders? Anyway, Shamp rejects his trophy, he prefers an abandoned subway station, and this closing dissonance may be the most illuminating aspect of *City-Solo*, so far as this author's later work is concerned. Later, her initiates earn their scars, but they, too, wind up ambivalent. No one simply cashes in and folds away the board.

To put it another way, the clown act of Gordon's debut arrives finally at serious feeling. What critical attention it's gotten has dwelt more on the off-kilter setting and fine-tooled language. Keith Waldrop, in a 2001 essay for *Context*, noted the many allusions, "classical, biblical, historical," and made comparison to earlier high-style exercises, like "[Thomas] Urquhart's Rabelais and [Richard] Burton's *Thousand and One Nights*." Gordon herself mentioned such "forebears," in a 1983 interview with *Gargoyle*. Our present perspective, however, reveals a more recent model for *City-Solo*, another shaggy-dog story from an author with a Baltimore base. That would be John Barth, close friend of John Hawkes, Gordon's mentor at Brown University. The obvious model for *City-Solo* would be Barth's 1960 novel *The Sot-Weed Factor*, a book that likewise foregrounds a baroque language. It makes mention of both Rabelais and Scheherazade; it puts a holy fool through madcap ups and downs. Yet Barth delivers his poet picaro to a decidedly ambiguous "success," and *Sot-Weed* ends up a love story, a work of serious feeling. Naturally, Gordon and Barth have many differences, but in order to understand what the younger author has gone on to do, it helps to see her first book's connection to another radical experiment that, on one filigreed sleeve, wears a bleeding heart.

She Drove Without Stopping, too, is a picaresque. What's more, its protagonist, Jane Turner, delivers a ringing peroration. About two-thirds of the way along, Jane reiterates the title clause several times as she bolts from Baltimore to L.A., struggling to break out of those rubbery comforts to which she was born:

> *She drove without stopping for twenty-four hours, midnight to midnight, except for a hypochondriacal consultation at a rundown one-pump station... [and afterwards] she drove off warily, trying to overtake her happiness now by sheer perseverance instead of velocity...*

Jane's middle name is Kaplan, she's Jewish on her mother's side, and she will never reach her Jerusalem, never overtake her happiness. The way she's been raised has set an impossible, ecstatic standard. Hardly have we met the girl than she reveals: "I masturbated every night from age beyond memory." At that point, the opening of the second chapter, the pleasure remains innocent, freed from "any sense that I was... pantomiming a conjunction of far more complex terms." It's Eden, where a girl goes naked unashamed and uses the personal pronoun.

But *Without Stopping* gets moving even while Jane's too young to drive. She's booted from Paradise by the violence of her father's first refusal to accept her kiss on the mouth. He's "not a criminal," Philip Turner, "not even a bad sort." Jane never suffers abuse, exactly. Yet Dad draws blood, the first time her love for him goes unrequited: "I was suddenly six feet away, blinking up at him, holding scraped elbows." After that, she's done with first person, for more than three hundred pages. The innocent becomes "the adventuress," in search of an alternative heaven.

Importantly, these adventures lack for anything surreal, outside of Jane's overheated mind. Even the brief passages above demonstrate how Gordon's second novel constitutes a departure *into the ordinary*, with one-pump stations and scraped elbows. Once Daddy and Mom divorce, once his rejected baby hits her teens, she acts out just as you might expect, "trying hard to be a bad girl." Not that her boyfriends aren't interesting, sharp-witted misfits beneath Jane's status. Not that her vicissitudes don't take an odd slant. I've never encountered so comic a rape as in *Without Stopping,* and the startled laughter kept coming throughout the Mutt-and-Jeff response of the police. Still, the system fails the girl in ways all too typical, and soon it feels like a "whole megilla." The rape's the turning point, actually. Wary of its "black cloud," Jane climbs into a rattletrap and drives without stopping. Only out by the Pacific, slinging booze in a dive bar and risking commitment to the faunlike Jimmy, artist and mystic and beach bum, can she have "her true adventure." Only there can she shake the false promise of her upbringing and come to terms with how "even an adventuress cannot choose her father, her first lover, the one least liable to be forgot."

The point is, Gordon's 1990 opus may be a grab bag, in which one page offers Jacob wrestling with the angel (Jane takes Hebrew lessons) and the next, *Brown v. the Board of Education* (she shares a homeroom with some of the first "colored" to attend her school), but, taken together, it reveals the outline of what once might've been acclaimed a parable of Women's Liberation. Jane travels amid '60s paraphernalia, there's even sort of a commune, but the majority of such details connect to the Civil Rights movement. The novel's first lines mention Martin Luther King, raising the idea of liberation, and providing specific historical context for this rematch of Yahweh and Lilith. In the climactic explosions, out in L.A., the most volatile elements are an African American and a Native American.

Yet the narrative never starts to feel like a political cartoon. Gordon's bravura style allows for no such broad strokes, and when this Eve makes her peace with the serpent, it's personal. For the final talk with Dad, the final break, she's once more using the pronoun "I." Still, Jane comes out of that conversation into a glaring reassertion of social and economic status, during a court hearing. The black whores around her all receive a thirty-day sentence, but Jane's public-drunkenness charge is quickly dismissed. The judge needs only one look at her "white skin, glasses, curly hair," to recognize her as "a child of the upper middle class. His class."

Indeed, isn't the protagonist's cross-country ride a "moneygreen Buick?" Doesn't she need the occasional small check from Dad? Even out West, she can't get free of "reproaches from the unimprisoned creature she might have been." She does publish her first poems, in a smudged and wacky venue, yet even this emblem of self-actualization takes her to economics. Her L.A. boyfriend may be a romantic hero, a starving artist—but after Jane sees print, she admonishes him: "I only started to be a poet so I wouldn't think it was my duty to pay your rent." A wonderful quip, one of many that raise the novel above simple diatribe. Feminism emerges, rather, like a monster from the id:

> *She could see what was coming. This would sweep her off to the world, which was suddenly altogether compelling and necessary, loaded as it was with human males. She would become a prowler...a centripetal force, with gravity in all her excentric orbs...From now on she would put herself into the hands of men without fear of disappearing, for she was the cunt from outer space.*

She Drove Without Stopping can feel like the "women's classic" that more famous cases hoped to be. Its heroine comes unshackled only to confront a fresh set of irons, heavier still, and so takes risks beyond those in, for instance, Erica Jong's *Fear of Flying* (1973). Too bad, then, that the book's *what* lacks the intelligence of its *how*. Its first third never quite transcends that predictable bad-girl pattern, the collapsing domestic circle and the child crazy to break out. Once Jane breaks out, too, some elements do seem drawn from a counter-culture scrapbook, such as her California boy. Nevertheless, in her first full-length fiction, Jaimy Gordon laid claim to the visionary knocking about, Bible-inflected, that American male writers have always taken as their entitlement. When the story fails to satisfy, it has to do more with limitations of the road novel than with those of the author.

*

After *Without Stopping, Bogeywoman* took ten years to appear. What-ever lay behind this long sabbatical (Sun & Moon Press may have been one of the most distinguished small presses, but of course it suffered the same lack of resources as all the others), the delay couldn't help but contribute to the author's obscurity. Yet the hiatus had a happier result too, namely that the novel turned out so well-made. Here Gordon solves the structural problem implicit in the previous book's title. Free of Kerouacian meandering, *Bogeywoman* confines its drama to three not-unfamiliar Northeast settings: a girl's forest camp in Maine, a psychiatric hospital in a bad Baltimore neighborhood, and the Great Dismal Swamp along Chesapeake Bay. It occupies a few eventful months of self-discovery for the 16-year-old Ursie Koderer. Ursie, Ursula, narrates a coming of age by way of coming out. Her first attempt at taking a woman lover leads her to disaster, but her sec-ond, while bumptious and terrifying, delivers her to (relative) safety. Indeed, the neatness of the drama proves surprising. A reader needs to step back to see how plausibly reaction suits action, in just a few key scenes, because the experience on the page seems all "humid longing," feverish in its mood swings: "All at once my heart opened up like a peacock's fan, I knew all the colors of love."

Now, that sentence pulls off quite a performance, with its active metaphor and surflike *all-all-l-l.* Yet the tone's serious, and while this seriousness suits the moment—Ursie's first meaningful encounter with Dr. Zuk, the woman who will save her—by far the majority of the well-turned phrases in *Bogeyman* traffic in laughter and surprise. The laughter may sag with pain, the surprise may pack a threat, but isn't such paradox natural to the best comedy? The novel brings off an open-throated new demotic, omnivorous in its attention to detail, especially sonic detail, and this constant celebration feels comic.

Consider the few lines leading up to the peacock moment. In these lines, the "you" is sister Margaret (the central figure in *Lord of Misrule*), on a visit to the psychiatric facility, Rohring Rohring. Maggie has come to persuade the younger Koderer to check out ("I know you're not buggy, Ursula"). To that end, she's giving her disheveled sib a haircut.

But Big Sister knows at once what's up, when she sees Ursie share a loaded look with Dr. Zuk.

> *Trouble dented your forehead. Your idled scissors snipped air, tinka tinka tink. Dr. Zuk, having blessed me with that look, was already squinching out the door in her silver sandals. I watched, the familiar systole diastole of her muscular buttocks, the flickering curves of her soccer player's calves. All at once my heart opened…*

Rich as this stuff is, here wiseacre description and there spellbound epiphany, it does without some of Gordon's most enchanting coinages. In particular, it does without "dreambox mechanic," *Bogeywoman*'s term for a psychiatrist. The expression occurs first in the opening lines, and it was mentioned in all the novel's few write-ups, though these tended to be brief (in *Publishers Weekly,* for instance). One can't help but wonder how many reviewers simply lacked the patience required for such neologisms to come clear. Gilbert Sorrentino blurbed the work as "radiant with energy…a radicalization of language," but it's just such language that tends to scare off a larger audience.

A shame, because *Bogeywoman* also deserves the encomiums that have to do with emotion, such as (in Sorrentino's case) "funny" and "bittersweet." Gordon's phrasing may suggest a Rube Goldberg contraption, but it's always in service to her character. Her opening evocation of "Camp Chunkagunk, *Tough Paradise for Girls*" feels moist, redolent, altogether woodsy, yet isn't such lush business appropriate to a 16-year-old who suddenly finds herself abrim with illicit desire? "From that moment," she declares on the second page, "I saw everything in a different light, murky, as through a dark lake. From then on I was a ✱ Unbeknownst To Everybody, and that was the meaning of Bogeywoman." The oversize asterisk looks queer, and the prose includes one or two other typographical oddities, tricks one might consider signs of postmodern experiment, the brand of fiction that's supposed to keep us from caring about characters. But then, the girl who dreamed up these off-the-wall constructions *is* queer. Ursie's far from the only gay teen to prefer living "unbeknownst." She's far from the only one to make a mantra of keeping mum: "Lemme die first."

To put it another way, Gordon has not lost touch with the ordinary. Ursie may speak in tongues, but we recognize the tomboy type, a "Wood Wiz" who loves "what a feast run amok the whole earth was." We understand when her first kiss and cuddle with another camper causes the "girlgoyle" to act out like the Kaplan Turner kid. She raises a great hue and cry over a tryst (hetero) between two of the staff, and they in turn discover what she has up her sleeves. The Bogeywoman has taken to self-mutilation. Such behavior lands her in the "bughouse," but it never gets in the way of sympathy.

Is it Ursie's fault, after all, that she's surrounded by such names, at once goofy and significant? Isn't she herself the bear in the woods, delighting in camp tales of "giant Gooskuk?" Then once the girl's goose is cooked, she's sent to a facility to assuage the Rohring Rohring in her head. This verbal gamesmanship (admirable in itself) is set off, always, by tragedy. Ursie can't be sent home from Chunkagunk, for instance, because her mother's dead and her father's on tour with his experimental troupe, Merlin's Puppets. And who's kept dancing at the end of the magician's strings, if not his daughters? Ursie and Maggie don't hate their performer Dad, but, "for Godzilla's sake," he can be distant.

Small wonder his younger daughter has been left hungry for "the feast of the world." Small wonder that, in the hospital, Ursie and others form a band, banging on homemade instruments and sending up cries for help. These are the Bug Motels, and their Kafkaesque torments also get a compassionate, though hilarious, fleshing out. Their songwriter is the Bogeywoman, and her greatest hit may be her piece for the anorexic heartbreaker Emily Nix Peabody, "refusal was her middle name."

Because I could not stop for lunch,
It kindly stopped for me.
The van read PIZZAS BY HASSAN
FAST FREE DELIVERY

...

It's two years later now and I'm
Still tryna put away
That eighteen-inch cold pizza
Known as immortality.

Again, the tomfoolery cuts unexpectedly deep, in its concern with outcasts. In the starveling Emily and in Emily Dickinson, in immigrant food and its on-the-fly counterfeit by other immigrants, the song dwells on the American fringe. Another in the Motels' repertoire tosses in, wouldn't you know it, a bit of Hebrew: "*Ma nishtanah* hullo whozat?" Also Ursie must negotiate favors with Reginald, "the Regicide," a very cool cat of an African American attendant. He enables her eventual escape with the help of two "Ayrabbers," the black ragmen who park their wagons across the street. By then, as Reginald puts it, the girl herself is "persona niggerata" around the facility. She may have killed one doctor and she's the underage lover of another. Dr. Zuk in fact has ducked into the wagon beside the girl, putting at risk (to say the least) her research fellowship from "Caramel-Creamistan."

The climax in *Bogeywoman* includes, to be sure, sexual climax. For the lovemaking the rhetoric rises but never loses its oddball integrity, such as the recurring reflection that Zuk's body is "like Central Asia." And by the time the runaways make it to the doctor's family lodge in the Great Dismal Swamp, where Zuk must sit down with her diplomat cousin and face the consequences of her infatuation—consequences that include Ursie's fortified sense of self—by that time, every incident is poised between comic and serious. The dialogue between Zuk and her cousin sounds as if it were lifted from *Duck Soup*. Gordon creates yet another demotic, but in their country homosexuality carries a death penalty. The swamp may recall good old Camp Chunkagunk, but here the Wood Wiz must pick her way between burning peatholes that could swallow her whole.

Has the girl come full circle? She's come out, among family and friends; she's no longer "Unbeknownst." Yet in acknowledging that hunger, has she brought on a new "hunger for difference"—meaning someone besides her Svengali? Ambivalence like that pervades the ending of *Bogeyman*. After the girl returns to Baltimore, she learns of the twins born to Reginald and one of his charges, the nymphomaniac of the Motels, and those twins embody duality: "boygirl, blackwhite, buggysane." As for their blackwhite, buggysane mother and father, they marry; their story has a happy ending. But what of the larger story? Was Zuk the crazy one, falling for love's fairytale? Once the doctor sees the error of her ways, she abandons the girl in the Great Dismal, where snakes crawl in the shadows and flames burst from the ground. It's an inferno, and the Bogeywoman's journey proves the reverse of Dante's. Starting out in a child's paradise, she moves on to a purgatory of souls in arrested development, and at last she achieves the hell of adult desire, gnashing its teeth while bound, inescapably, by rules and obligations.

Jaimy Gordon dares stand *The Divine Comedy* on its head and yet delivers a potent philosophical comedy all her own. The Bogeywoman may reconnect with family, she may make herself a place among the sane and straight, but she takes pride in the fading scars of her self-mutilation:

> *I think of my arms as my monster ticket...in case the whole world goes the monster way and monstrosity comes into its own. I'll be there. I'll be ready.*

She remains a warrior, even lying dormant. The novel closes *diminuendo,* as the grown girl coolly demystifies what she had with Zuk, and yet at the same time, she affirms her belief that, as her renegade lover put it, "*the heart is khan.*" So too, Ursie allows her older sister the final pungent summary of this magnificent novel's core value, in an adage appropriately Janus-faced: "an ounce of positive desire is worth a pound of negative regulation."

In *Lord of Misrule,* Gordon still flourishes postmodern colors. Throughout, she does without quotation marks, and the sex, while hetero, is all eyebrow-raising B&D. There's challenging vocabulary, like *xanthous* and *hierodule.* Early on appears a bit of American drug arcana, *goofer,* and many pages go by before a definition emerges. The word, in this context, refers to an herbal potion for hexing a horserace, a traditional magic among black grooms of the old South. The goofer's effect, however, is always unpredictable, and so too, remarkably, this novel casts an old-fashioned spell. Despite occasional devices that foreground experiment, *Misrule* impresses most in its command of story structure.

No longer does our author rely on a handmedown drama. Even *Bogeywoman,* as if to compensate for its brilliant *bizarrerie,* steers by the landmarks of initiation. A growth experience does figure prominently in *Misrule,* after Ursie's sister Maggie, "around 25 years old," arrives at Indian Mound Downs, a no-account track and stable in West Virginia. She learns the race game and gains the strength to break free of the rakish gambler Tommy Hansel. But then Hansel's in thrall himself, "challenged" by his girlfriend's "monkey-green eyes." The two young people, "bound in slavery of the man-woman kind," have fallen into sadomasochism, in scenes that match the trysts of *Bogeywoman* for their commingling of flesh and mind:

> *...had he read her mind? Maybe because he had that empty space where her own drawers and pigeonholes were stuffed with words, he often, spookily, out of a silence, echoed back to her her most treacherous thought...In an almost soothing gesture [he]...brought that hand down behind her, and suddenly he was binding both her hands together with the leather shank, then the chain.*

Maggie also very nearly joins Jane Turner as a rape victim. The novel's "monster," the hoodlum Joe Dale Biggs, slips her a horse tranquilizer. The young woman does get free, first from Biggs and later from Hansel, but she'd never have managed either without the intervention of an aging local relation known as Two-Tie. The nickname both suggests an angel's wings and picks up, lightly, the bondage metaphor.

Two-Tie's actual name is Jewish, we learn via clever indirection, and his connection to the Koderers is another of Gordon's brushes with that ethnic identity. Yet Two-Tie reflects mostly on his own Jewishness, not his relatives', and he never mentions the younger sister by name. In this novel, Maggie may carry the author's banner of Women's Liberation, but unlike Jane and Ursie, she's not the whole parade. She's not our sole vehicle of consciousness. *Misrule* also enters the personalities of Hansel, Two-Tie, and others, in roving third person. A few brief passages even seem to sample the wicked thoughts of Joe Dale Biggs—but those are actually another case of mind reading, courtesy of the novel's true protagonist, the weary racetrack veteran Medicine Ed.

One of the "old-timey negroes from down…in the hunt country," Ed offers sharp insights into everyone. Yet at 72 he finds himself closest to "Mr. Boll Weevil…*He's looking for a home. He's looking for a ho-me.*" The folk-song refrain not only provides pithy expression for the old man's tragic yearning but also places him at the head of Gordon's African American chorus. He's far more fully realized than *Bogeywoman's* "Regicide," or its "Ayrabbers," or any of the dark-skinned strays in *Without Stopping.* It's Ed who comprehends the "slavery" that binds "the frizzly hair girl" and "the young fool" with the "crazy look." It's Ed who provides essential background in the sport, the economics that underlie the drama. He knows about "goofers" too, from bitter experience; he's seen how fickle their magic can be. We share his regrets and refusals—he's sworn off magic, and booze along with it. We share what passes for his home, a half-crushed Winnebago decaying at the edge of Indian Mound. In Medicine Ed, *Misrule* brings off an act of imaginative sympathy that's nothing short of sensational.

The characters who make things happen, to be sure, tend to be younger. Just as old Ed suspects, Hansel's a hustler, with his own failing stable elsewhere in the state. He's come to Indian Mounds to cash in on a few of his horses; as unknowns, they'll run at long odds. As the scheme strays into complications, Gordon handles things with the skill of some racetrack-*noir* professional, another Dick Francis, scattering clues like a trail through the woods. But speaking of babes in the woods, doesn't this Hansel have a Gretel? Doesn't he think of Maggie (Margaret, Gretel), as a "long-lost twin," and doesn't the heroine wear her hair in braids? She likes to use the oven too, though she's "not the homey kind," rather "the restless, unsatisfied, insomniac kind." She's got a lot in common with Jane and Ursie, that is, as well as with the lost girl who kicked the cannibal witch into her own oven. So one night, as a pot of beans bubbles beside her, Maggie thinks how beans "were lots in the lottery for Lord of Misrule and his Lady, king and queen of Saturnalia, when the order of the world turned upside down." With that, she turns rightside up. No longer the child victim, she's "free to fly about the snowy skies on her broomstick."

Gordon may have become a pro at plotting, but her artistry remains complex. The touch of allegory, something else *Misrule* shares with its two predecessors, again gets treated with playful high-handedness. Maggie may escape destruction and come into power, but the journey proves bumpy indeed. After Biggs slips her a Mickey, as she fumbles for a way out, once again the author fetches laughs where you'd least expect: "She had to try, of course. Nowadays you couldn't just let some Black Bart tie you to the railroad tracks and walk away." So too, Lord of Misrule turns out to have a life outside the "drawers and pigeonholes" in Maggie's head, a rambunctious life, as a racehorse with a reputation for winning. Once the black nag arrives on the scene, Medicine Ed declares him "the devil." Who trucked Misrule in from Nebraska, after all, if not Joe Dale Biggs, that "monster in a labyrinth?" For the climactic race, monster and devil are in cahoots, Biggs intends to win, and he strong-arms the old trainer into breaking his vow and mixing up one more goofer. "I don't want no uncontrollable factors," the gangster snarls, and in that line this complex multivoiced narrative reveals a simple central irony. What could be more uncontrollable than magic?

The uproar at the novel's close proves apt, well-nigh supernatural, and it comes with a threat. This time it might be murder into the bargain, for Maggie. The final confrontation does resolve itself as comedy, again, and again distinctly Gordonian. Its blessings are mixed, and besides, the conclusion leaves us up in the air about the fairytale's ruling spirit, Medicine Ed. Has Ed found a home? The last pages are his, as were the first, but both show him working at the Downs and sleeping in the crippled Winnebago. Perhaps *home* requires a new definition, a metamorphosis, something like the way the natives reshaped the earth, building mounds to house the spirits. Or like the vision Maggie had whenever she groomed her horse:

> *...she knew...this one thing: She could find her way to the boundary where she ended and some other strain of living creature began. On the last little spit of being human, staring through rags of fog into the not human, where you weren't supposed to be able to see let alone cross, she could make out a kind of home.*

Love would be another term for it, this belonging beyond "the last spit." But *love* would be the more common term, hence pitted with cliché, and Gordon's careful with it in all three of her mature comedies. The happy ending never leads to the altar; not even Ursie gets her "girlgoyle." Rather, once this author outgrew her explorations in other genres (among which I'd include *Shamp*), she began delivering her women to mystery. They change, passing through those "rags of fog" we call myth and fable, the smoke that trails from all classic literature, but the ultimate shape of their metamorphosis remains "Unbeknownst." In this, the novels make a much-needed contribution to the American novel of a woman's self-actualization.

From the doomy brooding of Kate Chopin's *Awakening* (1899) through the sexed-up capering of Erica Jong, and from there on to the vengeful ferocity of Marge Piercy and the more complex cross-cultural materials of Louise Erdrich and others, fiction about a woman's place in the world has tended to omit the spiritual, the Unknowable. Instead such narratives emphasize social issues: political, economic, or otherwise. Erdrich's work provides the closest thing to an exception, and the best correlative for Gordon's. Granted, a novel so violent and admonitory as *Love Medicine* (1984) could never be called a comedy. Still, in that book and others, while Erdrich never ignores class or money or *Realpolitik,* no more than Gordon does, nonetheless she leavens their oppressiveness with magic and miracle, sometimes Christian, more often Lakota. In the process, she also risks formal experiments, at the level of both sentence and structure. She, too, had early exposure to John Barth, as a graduate of his program at Johns Hopkins, and her fiction demonstrates what he argued for in his "Exhaustion" and "Replenishment" essays: a postmodernism that can "have it both ways." The work, that is, both calls attention to the dream-making artifact in our hands and sweeps us up in a dream.

Still, Jaimy Gordon presents the more freewheeling case. Literature so potent as hers will outlast any cabal. Every story sustains a strong feminist element, and yet none collapse into lecture. Though the author can roar like the literary equivalent of a punk-rock Riot Grrrl, still she remains open to the least tenderness. And that tenderness may be a simple gesture of sisterly caring, ordinary as Baltimore, yet any gesture can set us wondering, with the Bogeywoman, "how many fantasticoes dare we hope…from any one family?"

John Domini's essay will appear in his forthcoming selection, The Sea-God's Herb, *on Dzanc Books. He has three novels, the latest* A Tomb on the Periphery, *two books of stories, and a number of grants and awards. See johndomini.com.*

Zacharis Award · Winter 2012-13

Zacharis Award *Ploughshares* is pleased to preset Heidy Steidlmayer with the twenty-second annual John C. Zacharis First Book Award for her poetry collection *Fowling Piece* (Triquarterly Books, 2011). The $1,500 award, which is named after Emerson College's former president, honors the best debut book by a *Ploughshares* writer, alternating annually between poetry and fiction.

This year's judge was John Skoyles, *Ploughshares'* poetry editor. In choosing the collection, Skoyles said: "Heidy Steidlmayer's *Fowling Piece* is marked by fiercely textured language and a humane voice. Its linguistic energy is perfectly matched by its calm and inquisitive tone, making a perfect tandem, an exact balance between writing and speech. The poems talk to the reader intimately while using an unexpected and often jolting diction, resulting in a collection both emotionally moving and formally inventive."

About Heidy Steidlmayer Other than an early comment from a "kind hearted teacher" that "the rhymes were supposed to be at the end of the lines and not right in the middle," the first profound poetic experience that Heidy Steidlmayer's remembers is reading Louise Bogan's poem "Cassandra" in college.

"I was an undergraduate in the writing program at Northwestern," she writes, "and Mary Kinzie had me look up the etymology of the word *silly* from the poem's first line, 'To me, one silly task is like another.' A whole world opened up for me when I discovered that *silly* originally meant 'happy' or 'blessed.'"

While she was working on the collection that became *Fowling Piece,*

Steidlmayer remembers coming across a picture of an old Tudor *lanthorn*. She was writing the poem "The X-ray," which begins "Mornings, the body's old / winter monochrome gives / its image of extraordinary cold / to a million hives—"

The lanthorn reminded her, she writes, "not only of a beehive but of a strange leather 'head.' This uncanny hive and its bees made me think of the structure of bones, their cells, where the bees going in and out were the living force—what the poet (and person intuits)—and what the X-ray does not show, but the poem does."

When asked how the poems connect to each together, Steidlmayer writes, "I think the one common element that these poems have is that the poems' subjects are in some ways trying to become language. The cuckoo wasps are curving into schwa, the praying mantis is reading an ancient Sumerian text, the butterflies transform like the beatitudes, and the blood of a saint of beginnings is flickering in its ampoule. In the illness poems, I think it is about a person trying to take in a profoundly "un-languaged" experience (for illness often offers in language's place its own coded blather—sagittal, cGy, T2 FLAIR, diffusion-weighted, gradient echo sequences, etc.—or varieties of clicks and thumps and whirs that masquerade as meaningful, and are meaningful in a nullifying kind of way—as in uh-oh, the radiation is coming on), but are all part of an experience so frightening and unthinkable that there is almost no existing in it, much less writing about it."

Inspiration comes from many places. In the natural world, she writes, "I feel a connection to things that extends far beyond what I could ever hope to understand myself." She also finds herself returning to the great anonymous poems, particularly "Beowulf" and "The Wanderer."

"When I write, sometimes I feel like I am trying to land a grand piano on a penny," Steidlmayer says. "I struggle to find the purest form of what the poem seems to want to say—with a kind of music that can be like Yeats' stone 'in the midst of all.'"

EDITORS' SHELF

Book Recommendations from Our Advisory Editors

Martín Espada recommends *Psalms of the Dining Room* by Lauren Schmidt: "The poetry of Lauren Schmidt does what poetry should do: make the invisible visible, indelibly, unforgettably. If ever a collection of poems embodied Whitman's dictum to speak for 'the rights of them the others are down upon,' this is it. The poet worked for several years as a volunteer at The Dining Room, a free meals program (what used to be called a "soup kitchen") in Eugene, Oregon. The poems inspired by the experience of working with this community—the poor, the unemployed, the physically and mentally disabled, veterans, the homeless—humanize the dehumanized, compelling us to see what we do not see and hear what we do not hear, to gaze upon the "ugly" until it becomes beautiful, to re-imagine, re-invent and repair the world. These are poems of lament, praise and thanksgiving; thus, they are truly psalms, and belong to that Biblical tradition. They also belong to the tradition of poets who have rolled up their sleeves to work among the damned, and have written from that perspective. In a cascade of miraculous images, vividly imagined, the poet moves from witness to visionary, expressing the sure knowledge that a vision of the impossible, expressed in the language of the possible, must precede any great change,

personal or political, intimate or global." (Wipf and Stock Publishers, December 2011)

DeWitt Henry recommends *Two, Two Lily-White Boys* by Geoffrey Clark: "In this classic story of male adolescence and homophobia, Clark writes with seemingly effortless clarity—clarity of narrative, sentence, meaning, and character—and this short, richly packed novel may well be his masterpiece." (Red Hen Press, 2012)

DeWitt Henry also recommends *Murdering the Mom* by Duff Brenna: "Brenna's childhood and coming of age are as harrowing as Maxim Gorki's, but where Gorki's vision calls for a Soviet revolution to free underclasses from the cycle of brutality, Brenna's celebrates our common humanity, complexity, and resilience, the revolution within. This is a memoir remarkable for its ironic acceptance of outrages." (Wordcraft of Oregon, 2012)

Tony Hoagland recommends Frank Bidart's *Watching the Spring Festival* and *Star Dust*: "I'm so glad that Bidart went back to writing the short poem—this is a form that makes the perfect housing for his remarkable powers of compression—syntactical, emotional, and intellectual. His intensity is phenomenal; his poems are the extreme yoga poses of consciousness in a war zone." (Farrar, Straus and Giroux, 2008 and 2006)

Maxine Kumin recommends *The Twelve Rooms of the Nile*, by Enid Shomer: "Gustave Flaubert and

Florence Nightingale meet as tourists in Egypt in 1849—historically, they were both there at the same time—and Shomer imagines the rich relationship that develops between them in an opulent 19th-century setting as they travel up the mysterious river. (Simon & Schuster, 2012)

Philip Levine recommends D. Nurkse's *A Night in Brooklyn:* "After I read D. Nurkse's last collection of poems, *The Border Kingdom,* I told myself there was no one in the U.S. who could write a better book. Well I was wrong, there was a poet who could and recently did publish a better book, the same D. Nurkse. *A Night in Brooklyn,* his newest collection, finds him on home territory—he was for a time the Poet Laureate of Brooklyn—he should be the laureate of the Western Hemisphere. He possesses the ability to employ the language of our American streets, shops, bars, factories, and any place else and construct truly lyrical poems, sometimes of love, sometimes of anger. He can be wonderfully large and inclusive: "In these long slant-lit streets, she says, / you will find factories that once made shoehorns, / waffle irons, or pearl cuff links and store front churches/ where voices adored the living God while tambourines / clashed a little behind the beat…" from "Twilight in Canarsie," which finally gets the poem it deserves. The voice behind these poems is certainly Nurkse's, but more often than not I feel it's that deepest voice we hear rarely if ever

and then only in poems, the voice of those closest to us, those we love and care for and who—because they are human—remain mysteries: "All my life I have been dying, of hope and self-pity, / and an unknown force has been knitting me back together." No one is writing more potently than this." (Alfred A. Knopf, 2012)

Margot Livesey recommends *The Beach at Galle Road* by Joanna Luloff: "In these beautiful stories set in Sri Lanka during the civil war, Luloff writes from the point of view of young and old, Americans and Sri Lankans. The result is an intricate web of stories that take us deep into a troubled place and time. I loved reading *The Beach at Galle Road* because of Luloff's profound grasp of her characters and her ability to show the ways, large and small, that they are all marked by the war." (Algonquin Books, October 2012)

Thomas Lux recommends *Cannoli Gangster* by Joey Nicoletti: "a gritty, funny, nervy book." (Turning Point Press, August 2012)

Thomas Lux also recommends *The Swamp Monster at Home* by Catherine Carter: "a poet with a great ear and a range from seriously hilarious to heart-breakingly serious." (Louisiana State Univ. Press, February 2012)

Thomas Lux also recommends *When Pianos Fall from the Sky* by Travis Wayne Denton: "quirky, highly imaginative poems with deep heart." (Marick Press, August 2012)

Antonya Nelson recommends *Stories for Boys* by Gregory Martin: "*Stories for Boys* is a charming and moving coming-of-age story, its narrator situated in the pivotal position between being his father's son and his sons' father. So refreshing and unique is Martin's treatment of the material that the reader will never mistake this book for its inferior competitors dealing with similar subjects (suicide, latent homosexuality, child abuse). One hopes this is the new wave of memoir: stories of people whose lives are not easily categorized nor dismissed. It is a sweet read." (Hawthorne Books, 2012)

Eleanor Wilner recommends *Wet* by Carolyn Creedon: "Out of fifteen years in what she calls 'the waitress wars' comes this book wet with the fluids of life—poems unashamed, pungent, gritty, and gorgeous, with a no-holds-barred honesty, a sacred sense of appetite, and a formal dexterity under the high-octane velocity, building cadence on cadence, simile on simile, until the whole world wears her kind of trouble, her wild and brilliant apprehension." (Kent State University Press, September 2012)

EDITORS' CORNER
New Works by Our Advisory Editors

Sherman Alexie, *Blasphemy: New and Selected Stories* (Grove Press, October 2012)

Anne Bernays, *The Man on the Third Floor,* a novel (The Permanent Press, November 2012)

Mark Doty, ed. (with David Lehman), *The Best American Poetry 2012* (Scribner, September 2012)

Martín Espada, *The Trouble Ball: Poems* (W. W. Norton, September 2012)

Marilyn Hacker, translator, *Tales of a Severed Head,* poems, by Rachida Madani (Yale University Press, October 2012)

Thomas Lux, *From the Southland,* nonfiction (Marick Press, March 2012)

Thomas Lux, *Child Made of Sand: Poems* (Houghton Mifflin Harcourt, November 2012)

Jay Neugeboren, *The Other Side of the World,* a novel (Two Dollar Radio, November 2012)

Maryanne O'Hara, *Cascade,* a novel (Viking, August 2012)

Gerald Stern, *In Beauty Bright: Poems* (W. W. Norton, September 2012)

Colm Tóibín, *The Testament of Mary,* a novel (Scribner, November 2012)

Dan Wakefield, ed., *Kurt Vonnegut: Letters* (Delacorte, October 2012)

Kevin Young, ed., *The Hungry Ear: Poems of Food and Drink* (Bloomsbury USA, October 2012)

Keith Althaus is the author of two books of poems: *Rival Heavens* (Provincetown Arts Press, 1993) and *Ladder of Hours* (Ausable Press, 2005). He has recently completed a book-length poem about the Ephrata Cloister. He lives in North Truro, Massachusetts, with his wife, the artist Susan Baker.

Valerie Bandura was born in the former Soviet Union. Her forthcoming collection, *Freak Show,* is slated for publication in May 2013 from Black Lawrence Press/Dzanc Books. Other recent poems have appeared in *Alaska Quarterly Review* and *Cimarron Review*. She teaches writing at Arizona State University, and lives in Arizona with her husband, fiction writer Patrick Michael Finn, and their son.

Ellen Bass' poetry books include *The Human Line* (Copper Canyon, 2007) and *Mules of Love* (BOA, 2002). Her poems have been published in *The Atlantic, The Kenyon Review, American Poetry Review, The Sun, The New Republic,* and other journals. Her nonfiction books include *The Courage to Heal* and *Free Your Mind.* She teaches in the MFA poetry program at Pacific University. ellenbass.com.

Ciaran Berry's first full-length volume, *The Sphere of Birds,* was published in 2008 by Southern Illinois University Press in North America and by The Gallery Press in Ireland and the U.K. His newer work has appeared recently in *AGNI, Crazyhorse, Gulf Coast,* and *The Threepenny Review.* He teaches at Trinity College in Hartford, Connecticut.

James Crews was born and raised in St. Louis, Missouri. His work has appeared in *Crab Orchard Review, Best New Poets 2006* and *2009, Columbia, Prairie Schooner,* and other journals. He is the author of three chapbooks: *Bending the Knot* (Gertrude Press Prize, 2009); *One Hundred Small Yellow Envelopes* (Parallel Press, 2009) and *What Has Not Yet Left* (Copperdome Prize, Southeast Missouri State University Press, 2010). His manuscript, *The Book of What Stays,* won the 2010 *Prairie Schooner* Book Prize in Poetry. He has worked as a salesman of bespoke wallpaper, an AmeriCorps VISTA volunteer and an English teacher in rural Oregon. He has an MFA from the University of Wisconsin-Madison and is now working on a PhD in Lincoln, Nebraska—which is actually a lot cooler than most people think.

Carl Dennis is the author of eleven books of poetry, most recently *Callings* (Penguin, 2010). A recipient of the Pulizer Prize and the Ruth Lilly Prize, he lives in Buffalo, New York.

Hilary Vaughn Dobel was raised in Seattle, Washington, and holds degrees from Princeton University and the University of Chicago, as well as an MFA from Columbia University in poetry and translation. Her work has also appeared in *Lana Turner*, and she currently resides in Cambridge, Massachusetts.

Peter Everwine's most recent books are *From the Meadow: Selected and New Poems* (University of Pittsburg Press, 2004) and *The Countries We Live In*, translations of Natan Zach (Tavern Books, 2011). He is the recipient of an American Academy of Arts and Letters Award in Literature, and fellowships from the National Endowment for the Arts and the John Simon Guggenheim Foundation. He lives in Fresno, California.

Kate Flaherty's stories and essays have appeared in *Creative Nonfiction, Brevity, Fourth Genre, Prairie Schooner, Louisville Review,* and elsewhere. "Heather, 1984" is from her manuscript, *My Brief History of Sex Education,* which is currently in circulation. Other writing and ranting can be found on her blog *Fact or Fiction* at kateflaherty.wordpress.com.

Shauna Galante grew up on Long Island and graduated from Emerson College in 2010. She lives in Portland, Oregon.

Barry Gifford's fiction, nonfiction, and poetry have been published in twenty-eight languages. "The Wicked of the Earth" is an excerpt from *The Roy Stories,* to be published October 2012 by Seven Stories Press/Random House. Gifford's books *Sailor's Holiday* and *The Phantom Father* were

each named a Notable Book of the Year by *The New York Times,* and his book *Wyoming* was named a Novel of the Year by the *Los Angeles Times.* His film credits include *Wild at Heart, Perdita Durango, Lost Highway, City of Ghosts, Ball Lightning,* and *The Phantom Father.* Barry Gifford's recent books include *Sailor & Lula: The Complete Novels* and *Sad Stories of the Death of Kings,* both from Seven Stories Press. He lives in the San Francisco Bay Area. For more information, visit www.BarryGifford.com.

Karl Taro Greenfeld is the author of six books, most recently the novel *Triburbia* (Harper), published in 2012. His fiction has appeared in *Harper's, The Paris Review, One Story, Best American Short Stories,* and *PEN/O. Henry Prize Stories.*

Ona Gritz's poetry has been published in numerous literary journals and anthologies. In 2007, she won the Inglis House poetry contest and the Late Blooms Poetry Postcard competition. In 2009, she placed second for *Lilith Magazine's* Charlotte Newberger Poetry Competition. Her chapbook of poems, *Left Standing,* was published by Finishing Line Press in 2005. Ona is also a children's author and columnist for the online journal, *Literary Mama.* She has received five Pushcart nominations for her work.

Barbara Hamby is the author of four books of poems, most recently *Babel* (2004) and *All-Night Lingo Tango* (2009), both from the

University of Pittsburgh Press. She was a 2010 Guggenheim fellow in Poetry and her book of short stories, *Lester Higata's 20th Century,* won the 2010 Iowa Short Fiction Award. She teaches at Florida State University and has new work in *American Poetry Review, Poetry, Five Points, Subtropics, AGNI,* and *The Yale Review.*

Kerry Hardie has published six full collections of poetry with The Gallery Press (Ireland), her most recent being *The Ash and the Oak and the Wild Cherry Tree* in 2012. Her *Selected Poems* was published by the Gallery Press in Ireland and by Bloodaxe in the U.K. She has also published two novels with Little, Brown, *A Winter Marriage* (2002) and *The Bird Woman* (2006), and is still trying to finish a third. She has won many prizes.

Gretchen E. Henderson is a Mellon Postdoctoral Fellow at MIT. Her books include the collaboratively-deforming novel, *Galerie de Difformité* (Lake Forest College Press, 2011); a critical exploration of literary appropriations of music and silence, *On Marvellous Things Heard* (The Green Lantern Press, 2011); a cartographic poetry chapbook, *Wreckage: By Land & By Sea* (Dancing Girl Press, 2011); and the recently published novel, *The House Enters the Street* (Starcherone Books, 2012). Gretchen received the Madeleine P. Plonsker Prize and currently is working on *Ugliness: A Cultural History* (for Reaktion Books).

Tony Hoagland's books of poems include *What Narcissism Means to Me* (Graywolf, 2003) and *Donkey Gospel* (Graywolf, 1998). He teaches at the University of Houston. Recently, he has founded *The Five Powers of Poetry* (fivepowerspoetry. com), a program for coaching high-school teachers in the teaching of poetry in the classroom.

Joshua Howes is an author and screenwriter. His fiction debuted in *Ploughshares* last year. He served as a Teaching Fellow and earned an MFA from Columbia University; as an undergraduate at Stanford, he won the Bocock-Guerard Prize for fiction. He has been a reporter for the Chicago Tribune, written the BET award-winning short film "Jackson Parish" (2009), sold his first feature script *Two Terrorists Meet* in 2012, and earned a National Golden Brad for his feature script *A House Divided.* Raised in Chicago, Howes lives with his wife in Manhattan, where he is writing a novel. Learn more at joshuahowes.com or reach out to him on Facebook.

Reese Okyong Kwon's writing has appeared in *The Southern Review, Kenyon Review, The Believer, American Short Fiction,* and elsewhere. She has been named one of *Narrative*'s "30 Below 30" writers, and has received scholarships and fellowships from Yaddo, Ledig House, and the Bread Loaf Writers' Conference. She lives in San Francisco, and can be found at reesekwon.com.

Brenna W. Lemieux has lived and written in Maryland, Pennsylvania, Illinois, Paris, and Galway. By the grace of various editors, her poems have appeared in *The Threepenny Review, North American Review,* and *Prairie Schooner.* She holds an MFA in poetry from Southern Illinois University Carbondale and currently lives in Chicago.

Matthew Lippman is the author of two poetry collections, *Monkey Bars* (Typecast Publishing, 2010) and *The New Year of Yellow* (Sarabande Books, 2007), winner of the Kathryn A. Morton Poetry Prize. He is the recipient of the 2010 Jerome J. Shestack Poetry Prize from *The American Poetry Review.*

Dave Nielsen was born and raised in Salt Lake City, Utah. He is a student in creative writing at the University of Cincinnati. His writing appears or is forthcoming in *The Massachusetts Review, Cutbank, American Literary Review,* and other magazines.

Matthew Neill Null's short fiction has appeared in *Oxford American* and *PEN/O. Henry Prize Stories 2011.* He has received fellowships from the Fine Arts Work Center, the University of Iowa, the Jentel Foundation, and the Michener-Copernicus Society of America. He lives in West Virginia, where he is working on a novel.

D. Nurkse is the author of ten books of poetry, including *A Night in Brooklyn,* published by Knopf in July 2012.

Rebecca Okrent's poetry has appeared in various publications including *The New Republic, Barrow Street, Western Humanities Review,* and several anthologies. Her poetry collection, *Squandered Sons,* will be published by Four Way Books in 2015.

January Gill O'Neil is the author of *Underlife* (CavanKerry Press, 2009), and a forthcoming collection, *Misery Islands* (CavanKerry Press, 2014). She is the executive director of the Massachusetts Poetry Festival and an assistant professor of English at Salem State University. She blogs at poetmom.blogspot.com.

Gretchen Primack's poems have appeared in *The Paris Review, The Massachusetts Review, Prairie Schooner, FIELD, Best New Poets,* and *The Antioch Review,* among other journals, and in a chapbook, *The Slow Creaking of Planets* (Finishing Line Press, 2007). She lives in the Hudson Valley, where she teaches and advises with the Bard Prison Initiative. Her website is www.gretchenprimack.com.

Grace Schauer is a graduate of the MFA program at Emerson College. She earned a BA in English from the University of Mary Washington and worked as an editorial assistant for two years before returning to school. A Florida native, she grew up outside Washington, D.C. Her poem "Seven Year Plan" recently appeared in *Breakwater Review.* She resides in Cambridge, Massachusetts.

Maria Terrone is the author of two poetry collections—*A Secret Room in Fall,* co-winner of the McGovern Prize (Ashland Poetry Press, 2006) and *The Bodies We Were Loaned* (Word Works, 2002)—and a chapbook, *American Gothic, Take 2* (Finishing Line Press, 2009). Her Pushcart Prize-nominated work has appeared in magazines including *Poetry International, Poetry,* and *The Hudson Review,* and in nearly twenty anthologies. Visit mariaterrone.com.

David Thacker's poems have appeared or are forthcoming in *Subtropics, The Cortland Review, Nimrod, Sycamore Review,* and elsewhere. He earned an MFA in poetry from the University of Idaho, where he was awarded the Academy of American Poets Prize. He currently teaches writing at the University of Idaho.

Emma Törzs lives in Missoula, Montana, where she writes and waits (tables). Her fiction has appeared in journals such as *Redivider* and *The Cincinnati Review,* and her poetry in the *Indiana Review.* Her work can also be found around the web in places like *Joyland, PANK,* and the *Tin House* blog. She is working on a novel about fear.

Ryan Vine's chapbook, *Distant Engines,* won a Weldon Kees Award and was published in 2006 by Backwaters Press. His honors include the Robert Watson Poetry Prize from *The Greensboro Review,* a Career Development Grant from the Arrowhead Regional Arts Council, and finalist nods for the *Black Warrior Review* Poetry Prize and the May Swenson Poetry Award from Utah State University Press. His poems and essays have appeared in *The American Poetry Review, Ploughshares, The Writer's Almanac,* and *The Minneapolis Star Tribune,* among other places. He's the Rose Warner Assistant Professor of English at the College of St. Scholastica in Duluth, Minnesota.

Xuan Juliana Wang was born in Heilongjiang, China, in 1985. She graduated from University of Southern California, received her MFA from Columbia University, and is currently a Wallace Stegner Fellow in fiction at Stanford.

Nance Van Winckel's sixth book of poems, entitled *Pacific Walkers,* will appear in spring 2013 with the University of Washington Press. She has poems recently out in *Kenyon Review, Massachusetts Review, jubilat, AGNI, West Branch, Gulf Coast,* and *FIELD.* A fourth collection of linked stories, entitled *Boneland,* which received a Christopher Isherwood Award, will appear in fall 2012 from the University of Oklahoma Press. She's received two NEA Fellowships in poetry and teaches in the Vermont College of Fine Arts' MFA in Writing Program.

Afaa Michael Weaver is a native of Baltimore, Maryland. He has received prizes for poetry and playwriting, including a Pushcart, Pew, and NEA fellowships, and the PDI Award in playwriting. His twelfth collection of poetry, *The Government of Nature*, will be published by the University of Pittsburgh press in early 2013. He holds an endowed chair at Simmons College as the Alumnae Professor of English, and is Director of the Zora Neale Hurston Center and Simmons International Chinese Poetry Conference.

Eric Weinstein received his AB from Duke University and his MFA from New York University. His poems have appeared in *Colorado Review, Denver Quarterly, Prairie Schooner, The Southern Review,* and other publications. He lives in New York City.

Stephen Neal Weiss has published poems in *Best New Poets* 2011, *Columbia Poetry Review, NewYorker.com,* and *42Opus,* and essays in *Gourmet, BlackBook, NewYorkMag.com, The New York Sun, Out,* and *Salon.com.* He received an MFA in poetry from NYU and is the former editor of *Yale Literary Magazine.* With his wife, Casey Kait, he is the author of *Digital Hustlers: Living Large and Falling Hard in Silicon Alley* (HarperCollins, 2001). They live with their children in South Orange, NJ.

GUEST EDITOR POLICY

Ploughshares is published three times a year: mixed issues of poetry and prose in the spring and winter and a prose issue in the fall, with each guest-edited by a different writer of prominence. Guest editors are invited to solicit up to half of their issues, with the other half selected from unsolicited manuscripts screened for them by staff editors. This guest editor policy is designed to introduce readers to different literary circles and tastes, and to offer a fuller representation of the range and diversity of contemporary letters than would be possible with a single editorship. Yet, at the same time, we expect every issue to reflect our overall standards of literary excellence.

SUBMISSION POLICIES

We welcome unsolicited manuscripts from June 1 to January 15 (postmark dates). All submissions postmarked from January 16 to May 31 will be returned unread. Submit your work at any time during our reading period; if a manuscript is not timely for one issue, it will be considered for another. Our backlog is unpredictable, and staff editors ultimately have the responsibility of determining for which editor a work is most appropriate. We accept submissions online. Please see our website (www.pshares.org) for more information and guidelines. Unsolicited work sent directly to a guest editor's home or office will be ignored and discarded.

All mailed manuscripts and correspondence regarding submissions should be accompanied by a self-addressed, stamped envelope (s.a.s.e.). No replies will be given by e-mail (exceptions are made for international submissions). Expect three to five months for a decision. We now receive well over a thousand manuscripts a month.

For stories and essays that are significantly longer than 5,000 words, we are now accepting submissions for *Ploughshares Solos* (formerly *Pshares Singles*), which will be published as e-books. Pieces for this series, which can be either fiction or nonfiction, can stretch to novella length and range from 6,000 to 25,000 words. The series is edited by Ladette Randolph, *Ploughshares* editor-in-chief.

Simultaneous submissions are amenable as long as they are indicated as such and we are notified immediately upon acceptance elsewhere. We do not reprint previously published work. Translations are welcome if permission has been granted. We cannot be responsible for delay, loss, or damage. Payment is upon publication: $25/printed page, $50 minimum and $250 maximum per author, with two copies of the issue and a one-year subscription. For *Ploughshares Solos,* payment is $250 for long stories and $500 for work that is closer to a novella.

time	space	support
3 years	*Austin*	*$27,500 per year*

MFA IN WRITING

THE MICHENER CENTER FOR WRITERS
The University of Texas at Austin

www.utexas.edu/academic/mcw
512-471-1601

THE
Rona Jaffe
Foundation
WRITERS' AWARDS

The Rona Jaffe Foundation identifies and supports emerging women writers. Recipients receive awards of $30,000.

2012 WINNERS

Julia Elliott
(fiction)

Rachel Swearingen
(fiction)

Christina Nichol
(fiction)

Kim Tingley
(nonfiction)

Lauren Goodwin
Slaughter *(poetry)*

Inara Verzemnieks
(nonfiction)

WWW.RONAJAFFEFOUNDATION.ORG

Layovers just got a lot more literary

THE KENYON REVIEW

Now available on the **amazon**kindle

PLOUGHSHARES SOLOS

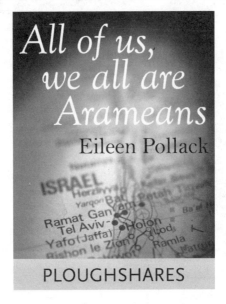

Digital-Only Single Essay Published Oct. 31, 2012

All Of Us, We All Are Arameans
by Eileen Pollack

Stuck with a plane ticket to Israel bought for her by a Polish Catholic ex-boyfriend, Eileen Pollack sets out on a hectic, solitary journey around the country, cataloging the region's rich history, natural beauty, and troubled politics, while examining her own complicated relationship to her Jewish faith and heritage. In this darkly comic, incisive, and nuanced essay, Pollack upends the reader's expectations, exploring her conflicted feelings of gratitude, dismay, and reverence. A travel essay filled with bewilderment, outrage, humor, and faith, "All of Us, We All Are Arameans" takes us on a trip that few American tourists would have the chutzpah to attempt.

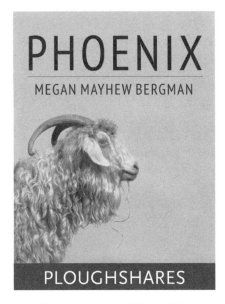

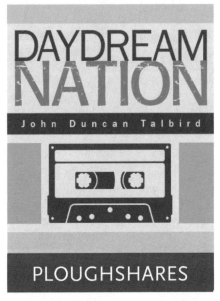

Digital-Only Single Story Published August 31, 2012

Daydream Nation
by John Duncan Talbird

The year is 1989 in Los Angeles, and Miles Jameson is about to graduate from high school. The last big party of high school is approaching, along with the end of a turbulent decade, and Miles has only a vague desire to "work with his hands" (his girlfriend points out that this is a bit trite). Marked with the disaffection and apathy that filled a particular era, and that has always marked adolescence, author John Duncan Talbird gives us a rollicking and bacchanalian look at the challenge of making something of yourself, even when it seems there is little to work with.

Available on nook & amazonkindle for $1.99

PLOUGHSHARES SOLOS

Digital-Only Single Story Published July 31, 2012

Lady of the Burlesque Ballet

by Timothy Schaffert

In a topsy-turvy ragtime era of side-shows and bamboo-zlers, Irish Maupin goes from street urchin to burlesque star. Plucked from the streets as a girl and fattened up for candy-factory advertising, she navigates a sensational career around heart-break and loneliness, gaining and losing hundreds of pounds, manipulated by the men around her even as she defies them. From acclaimed Nebraska author Timothy Schaffert, this inaugural Ploughshares Solo is a surreal adult fairy tale about obesity, murder, and how we change our bodies to meet the needs of others.

PLOUGHSHARES
LITERARY MAGAZINE

Did you know that we have a regularly updated blog with posts about writing and publishing from guest bloggers featured in this issue, plus book reviews and news?

✳

Join us online:
Blog: blog.pshares.org
Website: pshares.org
Stay connected:
Tweet @Pshares
Facebook.com/Ploughshares

✳

Also available on

PLOUGHSHARES

Stories and poems for literary aficionados

Known for its compelling fiction and poetry, *Ploughshares* is widely regarded as one of America's most influential literary journals. Most issues are guest-edited by a different writer for a fresh, provocative slant—exploring personal visions, aesthetics, and literary circles—and contributors include both well-known and emerging writers. *Ploughshares* has become a premier proving ground for new talent, showcasing the early works of Sue Miller, Edward P. Jones, Tim O'Brien, and countless others. Past guest editors include Richard Ford, Raymond Carver, Derek Walcott, Tobias Wolff, Kathryn Harrison, and Lorrie Moore. This unique editorial format has made *Ploughshares* a dynamic anthology series—one that has established a tradition of quality and prescience. *Ploughshares* is published in April, August, and December, usually with a prose issue in the fall and mixed issues of poetry and fiction in the spring and winter. Inside each issue, you'll find not only great new stories, essays, and poems, but also a profile on the guest editor, book reviews, and miscellaneous notes about *Ploughshares*, its writers, and the literary world. Subscribe today.

Subscribe online at www.pshares.org.

- -

☐ Send me a one-year subscription for $30.
I save $12 off the cover price (3 issues).

☐ Send me a two-year subscription for $50.
I save $34 off the cover price (6 issues).

Start with: ☐ Spring ☐ Fall ☐ Winter

Name _____

Address _____

_____

E-mail _____

Mail with check to: Ploughshares · Emerson College
120 Boylston St. · Boston, MA 02116

Add $30 per year for international postage ($10 for Canada).